Carnival Music in Trinidad

17,06

Carnival Music in Trinidad

∞

EXPERIENCING MUSIC, EXPRESSING CULTURE

∞

SHANNON DUDLEY

New York   Oxford
Oxford University Press
2004

Oxford University Press

Oxford   New York
Auckland   Bangkok   Buenos Aires   Cape Town   Chennai
Dar es Salaam   Delhi   Hong Kong   Istanbul   Karachi   Kolkata
Kuala Lumpur   Madrid   Melbourne   Mexico City   Mumbai
Nairobi   São Paulo   Shanghai   Taipei   Tokyo   Toronto

Published by Oxford University Press, Inc.
198 Madison Avenue, New York, New York, 10016
http://www.oup-usa.org

Library of Congress Cataloging-in-Publication Data
Dudley, Shannon.
   Carnival music in Trinidad : experiencing music, expressing culture / by Shannon
Dudley.
      p. cm.—(Global music series)
   Includes bibliographical references and indexes.
   ISBN 0-19-513832-5 (cloth : alk. paper) — ISBN 0-19-513833-3 (pbk. : alk. paper)
      1. Music—Trinidad and Tobago—History and criticism.   2. Carnival—
Trinidad and Tobago.   3. Trinidad and Tobago—Social life and customs.
I. Title.   II. Series.

ML3486.T7D83 2003
781.5'5—dc21

                                                                                            2003041941

Printing number: 9 8 7 6 5 4 3 2 1

Printed in the United States of America
on acid-free paper

GLOBAL MUSIC SERIES

General Editors: Bonnie C. Wade and Patricia Shehan Campbell

Contents

∞

Foreword

∞

In the past three decades interest in music around the world has surged, as evidenced in the proliferation of courses at the college level, the burgeoning "world music" market in the recording business, and the extent to which musical performance is evoked as a lure in the international tourist industry. This heightened interest has encouraged an explosion in ethnomusicological research and publication, including the production of reference works and textbooks. The original model for the "world music" course—if this is Tuesday, this must be Japan—has grown old, as has the format of textbooks for it, either a series of articles in single multiauthored volumes that subscribe to the idea of "a survey" and have created a canon of cultures for study, or single-authored studies purporting to cover world musics or ethnomusicology. The time has come for a change.

This Global Music Series offers a new paradigm. Instructors can now design their own courses; choosing from a set of case study volumes, they can decide which and how much music they will teach. The series also does something else; rather than uniformly taking a large region and giving superficial examples from several different countries within it, case studies offer two formats—some focused on a specific culture, some on a discrete geographical area. In either case, each volume offers greater depth than the usual survey. Themes significant in each instance guide the choice of music that is discussed. The contemporary musical situation is the point of departure in all the volumes, with historical information and traditions covered as they elucidate the present. In addition, a set of unifying topics such as gender, globalization, and authenticity occur throughout the series. These are addressed in the framing volume, *Thinking Musically* (Wade), which sets the stage for the case studies by introducing those topics and other ways to think about how people make music meaningful and useful in their lives. *Thinking Musically* also presents the basic elements of music as they are practiced in musical systems around the world so that authors of each case study do not have to spend time explaining them and can delve immediately into the particular music. A second framing volume, *Teaching Music Globally* (Campbell), guides teachers in the use of *Thinking Musically* and the case studies.

The series subtitle, "Experiencing Music, Expressing Culture," also puts in the forefront the people who make music or in some other way experience it and also through it express shared culture. This resonance with global studies in such disciplines as history and anthropology, with their focus on processes and themes that permit cross-study, occasions the title of this Global Music Series.

Bonnie C. Wade
Patricia Shehan Campbell
General Editors

Preface

∞

It was a privilege to be asked by the series editor, Bonnie Wade, to write this book on Trinidad's carnival music. My own relationship with Trinidad began in 1980 when I first played in a steelband at Oberlin College, where I was majoring in biology. Four years later I embarked on a much steeper learning curve, working as an apprentice to steel pan tuner Cliff Alexis. Cliff gave me an "old school" education in patience and respect, which laid the foundation for my subsequent graduate school training in ethnomusicology at the University of California, Berkeley (UCB). In 1989, I received a UCB graduate humanities grant for my first research trip to Trinidad, and between 1992 and 1994 I conducted more extensive research on Trinidadian steelband music, funded by a Fulbright dissertation grant. My most recent field research on Trinidadian carnival, in 2000, was funded by grants from the Simpson Center for the Humanities and the Royalty Research Fund at the University of Washington, where I currently teach.

In Trinidad I received generous assistance from Pan Trinbago, the University of the West Indies, the National Broadcasting Service, Radio Trinidad, the National Carnival Commission, the National Archives, and several steelbands I was privileged to play with, including Pandemonium, Phase II Pan Groove, Hummingbird Pan Groove, Bird Song, and Our Boys. Other individuals to whom I am particularly indebted for their help and inspiration include my wife, Marisol Berríos-Miranda; Patrick Arnold; Godwin Bowen; the late Carleton "Zigilee" Constantine; Alvin Daniell; Lloyd Gay; Rawle Gibbons; Ray Holman; Kim Johnson; Michael Robinson; Owen Serrette; Jit Samaroo; and Len "Boogsie" Sharpe. But this book could not have been written without the help of *many* other musicians and music enthusiasts, too numerous to list here, who gave of their time and knowledge, and whom I thank from my heart. Finally, for their help in the arduous task of procuring permissions for the musical examples, I am grateful to Nicky Inniss and David

Bereaux at the Copyright Organization of Trinidad and Tobago, Tim Allen at Integrated Copyright Organization, Jean Michel Gibert at Rituals Music, Eddie Grant at Ice Music, Daniel Sheehy at Smithsonian Folkways, Lutalo Masimba at the Trinidad Unified Calypsonians Organization, Rounder Records, Simeon Sandiford, Granville Straker, David Rudder, Rikki Jai, Sandra Devines, Denise Belfon, and Carlyle Roberts. To all these friends and colleagues, I have tried my best to write a book that is worthy of your music and your generosity.

CD Track List

∞ To find and purchase these recordings, see Resources, pp. 109-112 and visit: www.oup.com/us/globalmusic

1 "Pump Up," Austin Lyons (Superblue). ℗ & © 2000 Rituals Music.
2 Chant to Osanyin, performed by Babalorisha Clarence Forde and members of the St. Francis Shrine, Tacarigua, Trinidad. © 2000.
3 "Tassa drumming," the Corcoree band. © 1999 Rounder Records.
4 "Calinda," Tamboo from *Bamboo-Tamboo, Bongo and Belair*, Cook 05017, provided Courtesy of Smithsonian Folkways Recordings. © 1956. Used by permission.
5 "Iron Duke in the Land," Julian Whiterose. 1914.
6 "Jean and Dinah" the Mighty Sparrow (Slinger Francisco). © 1956.
7 "Jean and Dinah," from the recording entitled *Jump-Up Carnival/ Calypso Tent*, Cook 01072, provided Courtesy of Smithsonian Folkways Recordings. © 1956. Used by permission.
8 "Chauffer Wanted," the Mighty Chalkdust (Hollis Liverpool). © 1989 COTT.
9 "High Mas'," David Rudder. © 1998 COTT.
10 "Caribbean Man Part 2," Christophe Grant, Sandra Devines (Singing Sandra). © 2000.
11 "Congo Bara," Keskidee Trio. 1935.
12 "Pan in A Minor," Aldwyn Roberts (Lord Kitchener). © 1986.
13 "Back Line," Phase II Pan Groove. © 1986.
14 "Back Line," demonstration of different parts. Performed by students and faculty at University of Washington.
15 "Pan in A Minor," Renegades Steelband. © 1987.
16 "Cyar Take That," Brother Resistance. ℗ & © 1996 Rituals Music.
17 "Burnin'," Denise Belfon. ℗ & © 2000 Rituals Music.
18 "Dulahin," Rikki Jai. © 1998 COTT.

CHAPTER 1

Carnival and Society

∽

It is Tuesday afternoon in Port of Spain. I am moving along Tragarete Road behind a flatbed truck loaded with huge speakers, surrounded by masqueraders dressed in sequined bikinis and dazzling headdresses (Figure 1.1). They are members of a masquerade band called Streets of Fire, and, since they already have passed the judging points, they no longer are concerned about noncostumed infiltrators such as myself detracting from their spectacle. The DJ's music is so loud that I can feel my internal organs shaking with each thump of the bass. I've given up trying to protect my hearing and have surrendered to the power of the soca music, "chipping" (stepping in time) and swaying down the road with everyone else. We are dancing to a song by the calypsonian Preacher, who seems to be singing about fruit. The dancers relax with the slow, funky groove and smile suggestively as they sing the chorus: "Two sapodilla and a nine-inch banana—what she want, what she want." After a while, a faster beat begins to sound, and Preacher's song fades, giving way to Super Blue's "Pump it Up" (CD track 1). A new energy transforms the dancers. They jump when Super Blue breaks the rhythm on the words, "I wish I could, I wish I could, I wish I could" and respond with a fury of winding waists as the rhythm returns with, "wine on you!"

Spectators line the street, watching the beautiful mas' (masquerade). As one DJ truck passes and moves down the road, another truck approaches, followed by a different section of the band. Bystanders are thus enveloped in an unbroken flow of earth-shaking sound for as long as it takes the whole band (six or eight sections) to pass, and many dance in place as they watch. Vendors peddle roti (curry wrapped in a kind of unleavened bread fried on a skillet), pelau (rice with pigeon peas), fried chicken, hot dogs, soft drinks, beer, and rum. Food wrappers, cans, and bottles mingle in the gutter with feathered headdresses, glittering mantles, and other abandoned pieces of costumes (of which my five-

FIGURE 1.1 *Members of the band Streets of Fire. This is a "fancy mas'" band in which the participants purchase costumes based on sketches advertised by the designer.*

year-old daughter has by now made a fabulous collection), the discarded remains of two days of intense spectacle and fun.

At the corner of Cipriani Boulevard I spot Invaders steelband. In contrast to Streets of Fire's glitzy and flesh-revealing costumes, the masqueraders with Invaders are wearing sailor uniforms (Figure 1.2). The musicians are taking a rest and waiting for Streets of Fire to pass because they know their steelband can't be heard over the booming sound of the DJ trucks. They stand behind steel pans that are mounted on a truck bed, five feet above the road. At this height some of the band's sound gets lost, but Invaders no longer can find enough supporters to push pans on wheeled racks at ground level, as they once did.

I decide to leave Streets of Fire and go with Invaders. The steelband is returning to its panyard, where everyone will rest for a while before going out at night for the "last lap" along the Western Main Road in the neighborhood of St. James. The house I'm staying at is close to the panyard, and I need a rest, too. When the DJ trucks have passed, the steelband starts up again, playing an arrangement of Julio Iglesias Jr.'s "Bailamos." The warm strumming of the pans and the *tingi licki, tingi*

FIGURE 1.2 *People playing sailor mas' with Invaders steelband. These hats and T-shirts are very simple and inexpensive sailor costumes compared to the elaborate military attire or "fancy sailor" extravaganzas that were popular in the heyday of the steelbands in the 1950s and 1960s.*

licki of the irons swing beneath the romantic melody and make our feet light as we chip along the road toward home. . . .

∞

Musical performances like these can be understood in many ways: as spectacle and festivity, as social processes and institutions, as expressions of identities and ideas, and as crafts with long histories and diverse roots. To understand musical performances in all these dimensions one obviously needs to pay attention to more than just musical sounds. In this book I frame Trinidadian carnival music in terms of three interrelated issues that cut across musical genres: tradition, social identity, and performance context/function.

Tradition is a word whose meaning may be more complicated than it seems. Most people understand tradition to mean a practice that people of a certain community (e.g., family, town, nation, or religious faith) observe in the same way year after year and that affirms the continuity of that community's bonds and culture. Because carnival traditions are meaningful to Trinidadians in this sense, it is important in a book like this to look at aspects of continuity in carnival music, such as the value placed on word play in calypso (Chapter 2) or the assertion of lower-class pride and power through carnival performances like steelband music (Chapters 1 and 4). On the other hand, carnival music traditions are not passed simply from one generation to the next, but are constantly constructed and reconstructed through performance, promotion, staging, sponsorhsip, recording, and broadcast. In Trinidad, one especially important way for people to define and validate tradition is formal competition (Chapters 1 and 5). Debates about tradition and innovation are also encoded in the naming of new styles, such as rapso or chutney soca (Chapter 6). The label of "tradition" may be used to privilege one view of culture over another; for example, Trinidadians of Indian descent sometimes resent the promotion of calypso and steelband music as an attempt to privilege Afro-Trinidadian culture as the national culture (Chapters 1 and 6).

As the last example shows, the performance and patronage of music help to articulate *social identiy*. Social identity is linked to tradition in two important ways: (1) the continuity of tradition affirms community, and (2) the reinvention of tradition responds to contemporary concepts of class, ethnicity, nation, age, gender, and so on. For example, some genres, such as ragga soca (Chapter 6), appeal to generational identity (just as must of us can probably think of music that we listened to in high school that distinguished us from our parents). Where once the class identity of the steelband was a barrier to participation for middle-class youth, in more recent years the steel pan has become a symbol of national identity, encouraging the participation of a broader range of class and ethnic groups (Chapter 4). National identity is defined not only in terms of the inclusion of various classes and ethnic groups within Trinidad and Tobago, but also in relation to the cultures of other nations, as can be seen in debates about foreign influences in steelband music (Chapter 5) and in calypso and soca (Chapter 6). Thus through listening to music, and to the way people talk about and value music, we may learn something about how people see their place in society and in the world.

A third issue that runs through these chapters is *performance context and function*. All of the musical genres discussed here are conditioned in important ways by their functions, which include dance, storytelling, social protest, rivalry, spectacle, and entertainment. Attention is given throughout this book, therefore, to the way music functions in the context of its performance. Chapter 3, for example, describes how calypso music for dancing on "the road" differs in important ways from calypso performed for seated audiences in "tents." At the most general level, of course, the performance context for all the genres discussed here is carnival. I therefore begin in this chapter with an explanation of Trinidadian carnival, its social history, and its performance traditions.

CARNIVAL

Carnival in Trinidad—specifically the celebration that takes place in the capital city of Port of Spain—is one of the best-known and heavily attended carnivals in the world; it is imitated in many other celebrations, including Brooklyn's Labor Day festivities, Toronto's Caribana, and London's Notting Hill Carnival. Trinidadian carnival also has given rise to art forms that have spread beyond the boundaries of the island and have developed, to differing degrees, independently of carnival: calypso has been influential throughout the Caribbean, North America, England, and Africa; steelbands are taught in schools all over the United States and Europe; and Trinidadian mas' men (masquerade designers) have also made an international impression, one of the most striking examples being Peter Minshall's giant puppets and other creations for the opening and closing ceremonies of the Olympics.

There are, of course, carnivals with histories that are quite independent of Trinidadian carnival, including Mardi Gras in New Orleans, Carnaval in Brazil, and other carnivals throughout Europe and the Americas. Although the scheduling of carnival has been adjusted in some of the smaller Caribbean islands to attract tourists, in North America to accommodate the weather, and in communist Cuba to celebrate the revolution, the festival called "carnival" is traditionally tied to the Christian calendar. The word derives from the Latin *carne vale*, meaning "farewell to meat," because the celebration of carnival precedes the forty days of fasting and penance that culminate in Easter. Carnival is a period of drinking, feasting, and fun that ends suddenly on Ash Wednesday, the beginning of Lent (hence the term Mardi Gras, French for "Fat Tuesday"). Although Lent and Easter are observed by all Christians, carnival is associated mainly with Catholic nations.

Carnival is not, however, a church-sanctioned institution. Indeed, in Europe it is said to have functioned as an outlet for pagan fertility celebrations that the Catholic church relegated to the pre-Lenten period. Similarly, in the Spanish, Portuguese, and French colonies of the Americas, carnival was a time when special license was granted for African and indigenous peoples to express their traditions of music, dance, and masquerade—and to invent new ones. While linked in name to an international festival, therefore, Trinidadian carnival must be understood as the product of Trinidadian creativity and in relation to Trinidad's unique social and political history.

TRINIDADIAN SOCIETY

Trinidad lies close off the northeast coast of Venezuela, the southernmost island in the Antilles, or Caribbean, islands (Figure 1.3). Measuring roughly fifty by thirty miles, the island has a population of just over 1 million people. Along with the smaller island of Tobago to its north, it has constituted the independent nation of Trinidad and Tobago since 1962. Trinidad and Tobago is one of the most prosperous nations in the Caribbean because of its petroleum reserves; it is also one of the most culturally diverse. The original inhabitants of Trinidad were the Arawaks, who first encountered Europeans when Christopher Columbus claimed their island as a Spanish colony in 1498 and called it "Trinidad" for the group of three mountain peaks he had seen as he approached from the south. Many of the Arawaks died of diseases that the Europeans communicated to them, and their society and culture were virtually obliterated during the following centuries of colonial exploitation. The Arawaks were largely replaced by European colonists (first Spanish, then French and English) and the laborers they imported from all over the world (especially Africa and India) to fuel a plantation economy. Different ethnic groups sometimes still are identified with the economic niches they filled in colonial Trinidad.

Like many of the Caribbean islands, Trinidad has a large population of people whose ancestors came from Africa. Most Africans came to Trinidad as slaves brought by force from their homeland, or from other Caribbean islands, to cultivate crops that were grown on large plantations for export to Europe: tobacco, coffee, cotton, cocoa, and, most importantly, sugar. Some Africans also came after the era of slavery as indentured laborers or free travelers. People of African descent commonly are referred to in Trinidad as *black* or *creole* (a word that has other meanings also, explained later) or, in more formal speech and in writing, as African or Afro-Trinidadian.

There is an equally large population of people whose ancestors came from the Indian subcontinent. These people are usually referred to simply as *Indian*. Most of them came to Trinidad in the latter half of the nineteenth century to replace slave labor after the 1838 Emancipation.

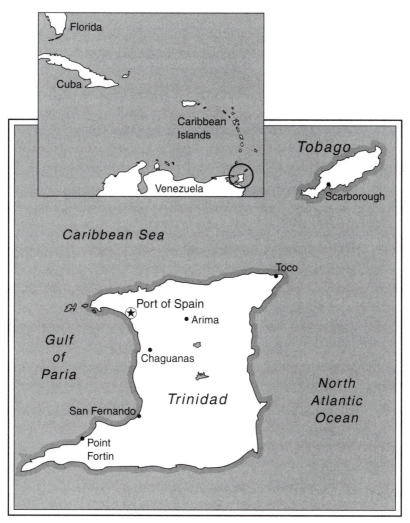

FIGURE 1.3   *Trinidad.*

They were brought to the Caribbean through an arrangement known as *indentureship*, in which workers received free passage in exchange for a contractual obligation to work in Trinidad for a specified period of time. Unlike slaves, indentured laborers were paid wages and were eventually freed, commonly after five years, but they often suffered extremely difficult working and living conditions. While the economic roles of Indo-Trinidadians have diversified immensely, their population is still most concentrated in the central part of the island, where sugar cane is grown. Afro-Trinidadians and Indo-Trinidadians together constitute roughly 80 percent of the population in Trinidad today.

Members of the remaining 20 percent or so of Trinidad's population would describe themselves either as mixed race or as belonging to one of several other ethnicities. Many Arabs came to Trinidad as cloth merchants during the colonial period, and their descendants commonly are referred to as *Syrian*, even though many trace their ancestry to other Middle Eastern countries, such as Lebanon or Jordan. There is also a sizeable community of *Chinese* in Trinidad, some of whom are descended from indentured laborers who came in the nineteenth century, and others who have arrived only recently to work in small businesses, especially restaurants. A fairly cohesive *Portuguese* community is descended from immigrants who got their start in Trinidad as grocers and shopkeepers. And while the first Europeans to colonize the island were from Spain, Trinidadians who are called *Spanish* today are more likely to be descended from Spanish-speaking Venezuelans than from Spaniards; in the countryside they sometimes are called *coco payol* (cocoa español), because many Venezuelans came to Trinidad to work on cocoa plantations.

The term *white*, in Trinidad as in many other places, refers to people of European descent, but many white Trinidadians retain more specific identities. Portuguese (or even Syrians) sometimes might be called white, but, because they never represented a colonial power, they have a different status than the English and French do. A few older Trinidadians were born in England, and many others are descended from English parents or grandparents. Trinidadians of French descent tend to come from families who have a longer history in the island, many tracing their Trinidadian roots to the eighteenth century. They may be referred to as *French creole*, but today this term is less ethnically specific than it was in the nineteenth century, and it tends to connote people of any European ancestry (the term *creole*, or *criollo* in Spanish, refers in many parts of the Americas to people of European descent born in the New World). French creoles and English owned most of the land in colonial Trinidad and dominated big business, international trade, and banking. Since independence, other ethnic groups have aquired land and integrated these and other industries, and white privilege no longer can be assumed. Nonetheless, whites in Trinidad (who constitute only about 1 percent of the population) still have disproportionate financial power and belong almost exclusively to the middle and upper social classes.

While Trinidad's class structure is rooted in distinctions of color and power, with light-skinned French and English managing at the top and dark-skinned Africans and Indians laboring at the bottom, this hierarchy is complicated by culture. On the one hand, people of different ethnicities and classes share many cultural practices. Americans may be surprised, for example, to hear whites or Chinese from Trinidad speaking with a "Caribbean" accent. Afro-Trinidadians eat Indian curry and roti, and Indo-Trinidadians dance to creole soca music at carnival. Trinidad does not have the degree of separation between races and ethnic communities that one finds in the United States. People of different ethnicities live and work side by side in Trinidad, especially in large cities like Port of Spain and San Fernando.

On the other hand, cultural differences create significant divisions even between people who share a similar economic and social status. Afro-Trinidadians and Indo-Trinidadians, for example, often see themselves in different cultural terms. Afro-Trinidadians tend to conceive of their culture as "Trinidadian" or "creole," born of fusion and reinvention in the Caribbean (another common meaning of the term *creole*). Indo-Trinidadians also see themselves as Trinidadian, but, compared to Afro-Trinidadians, they maintain a stronger identification with their place of origin through religious practices (mainly Hinduism), language (Bhojpuri is still spoken by some older Indo-Trinidadians, and younger people often are familiar with modern Hindi through Indian cinema or even formal instruction), and the arts (e.g., Indian films). Partly because Indo-Trinidadians were less eager for independence and nationhood in the mid-twentieth century, Afro-Trinidadians initially dominated Trinidadian politics.

The People's National Movement (PNM), which held power from 1962 until 1995 (with a brief interruption in the late 1980s), was a political party with a predominantly Afro-Trinidadian constituency. Indo-Trinidadians have made more impressive strides in the economic realm, and they recently gained political influence with the electoral victories of the United National Congress (UNC). Nonetheless, decades of PNM political domination and government sponsorship of carnival reinforced the place of the Afro-Trinidadian carnival arts as the "national" arts of Trinidad and Tobago—a conception of "Trinidadian culture" that leaves many Indo-Trinidadians feeling left out. Brief mention of Indian musical genres is made in this chapter and in the final chapter of this book. Because I have chosen to focus on carnival music, however, I mainly discuss Afro-Trinidadian performance traditions.

TRINIDADIAN CARNIVAL IN THE NINETEENTH CENTURY

The cultural friction between Afro-Trinidadians and Indo-Trinidadians has a parallel in the nineteenth-century mistrust between French creoles and the English. The first Europeans to settle in Trinidad in large numbers were French planters, who came to Trinidad between 1783 and 1797 at the invitation of the Spanish king, Charles III. The Spanish, concerned with filling the colony with as many subjects as possible, reasoned that French Catholics could be persuaded to obey the Catholic king of Spain. The king's offer of free land attracted many French planters, who came from islands such as Haiti and Martinique, bringing slaves with them. Despite this increase in Trinidad's Catholic population, the English took military control of Trinidad in 1797; planters and slaves from the French Caribbean, however, continued to exert a dominant cultural influence in Trinidad. Until the beginning of the twentieth century, for example, the majority of Trinidadians spoke *patois* (a mixture of African languages and French). Another important French influence was carnival, and efforts by the English to suppress carnival celebrations during the nineteenth century created some fascinating fractures in the hierarchy of color and class.

Emancipation of the slaves in 1838 (the process actually began in 1834, initiating an odd period of "apprenticeship") brought about significant Afro-Trinidadian participation in carnival and led to a split between the public carnival in the street and private carnival celebrations staged in restricted venues of the social elite. Lower-class Afro-Trinidadians took to the streets in carnival bands that were sometimes patterned on European royalty, with kings and queens and courtiers. These bands, or "regiments," were organized along linguistic lines, and confrontations between French- and English-identified bands frequently erupted in violence. Other masqueraders portrayed a variety of individual characters who ranged from humorous to threatening: for example, Dame Lorraine (a man who portrayed a fat, bawdy woman), pisse en lit (a man dressed as a woman, or sometimes a woman who sought to offend through various obscene and vulgar displays), Pierrot (an elegantly dressed character who challenged rivals in formal speeches and battled with a whip or stick), and many kinds of devils (Figure 1.4), who took delight in entertaining, offending, and frightening the public.

The lower-class people who participated in these revels, particularly the women, were referred to as *jamettes* (from the French word *diametre*, describing people who are beyond the "boundary" of respectability), and many upper-class people viewed the *jamette* carnival not only as offensive, but also as a threat to public order. The English colonial administration, which was mistrustful of festivity in general, already had instituted martial law at Christmastime beginning in 1800. After the 1838 Emancipation they also limited carnival celebrations to the Monday and Tuesday before Ash Wednesday, a schedule that still is observed in Trinidad today. This is why the opening of carnival in the wee hours of Monday morning, or *j'ouvert* (pronounced "joo-vay," from the French *jour ouvert*), is still the most intense expression of disorder and anarchy in Trinidadian carnival, marking the lifting of official restrictions on public assembly and behavior (Figure 1.5).

FIGURE 1.4   *These devils have smeared their bodies with oil and blue powder and provide musical accompaniment with vehicle brake drums, or "irons," which they play in interlocking patterns (see Activity 4.3 for an example of an interlocking pattern).*

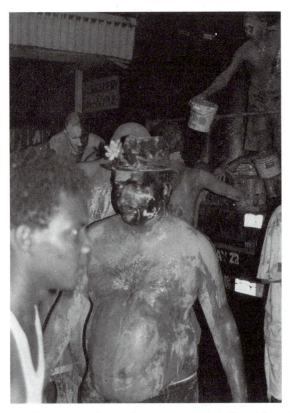

FIGURE 1.5. *J'ouvert morning revelers smearing their bodies with mud and grease paint.*

Fear and resentment of the *jamette* carnival increased through the nineteenth century and came to a head in the infamous Canboulay Riot of 1881. *Canboulay* (from the French *cannes brulées,*" meaning "burned cane") was a re-enactment of the forced marches that slaves endured when a cane field burned and had to be harvested instantly with the help of slaves from neighboring plantations. After emancipation this kind of torchlight procession was resignified as a way for Afro-Trinidadians to claim public spaces and attention, and it became a regular (and somewhat volatile) feature of carnival. Canboulay processions sometimes were associated also with a kind of stick-fighting called *kalenda*. Each neighborhood in the poor areas of Port of Spain had its own *kalenda* band, led by a *chantwell* who sang songs of challenge and boasting, accompanied by drummers and a chorus. Confrontations between bands usually began as song duels between the *chantwells* but often escalated into stick battles that could result in serious injury or death. Concerned about this violence and about the general disorder of carnival, a new police captain named Baker planned in 1881 to put a stop to the Canboulay procession. Stick-fighters from different bands joined forces against Captain Baker and waged a pitched battle with the police that lasted for hours on carnival Monday night. The Canboulay Riot has become the most well-known symbol of Trinidadian carnival's potential for resistance of and rebellion against authority.

In addition to its demonstration of black lower-class solidarity, one of the most interesting consequences of the Canboulay Riot was the outrage of the French creoles. Many of them thought Captain Baker's tactics were excessive, and they saw the police actions as a sign of disrespect for a festival that they strongly identified with themselves. To appease these influential citizens, the English governor confined police to their barracks the following day, dramatically underlining an alliance of common interests between the *jamettes* and the elite French creoles. This alliance also extended into the realm of the aesthetic, as daring young upper-class men (known as "jacket men" for their fine clothing) actually participated in some of the *jamette* carnival activities, including stick-fighting, in the late nineteenth century. United by their mistrust of the English authorities and their enjoyment of carnival, the *jamettes* and the French creoles defended carnival against the authoritarian impulses of the English colonial government.

One of the most important strategies in this defense was the organization of formal competitions for masquerade and music, which began around 1900. Prizes of cash and merchandise were supplied by businessowners who saw the competitions as a chance to advertise and boost sales of expensive costume materials. Carnival lovers supported the competitions as a way of establishing the status of carnival masquerade and music as legitimate and sophisticated art forms, thus making it harder for conservatives to ban carnival. The flip side was that many of the supposedly "distasteful" conventions of the *jamette* carnival were excluded by the judging criteria. Courtier costumes, for example, were privileged over painted devils, and violins and guitars were privileged over bamboo stamping tubes and bottle-and-spoon percussion.

Another result of the effort to make carnival performances more "respectable" was the marginalization of women performers. While women had a prominent role in the nineteent--century *jamette* carnival, competitions and official promotion during the twentieth century tended to discourage their participation, especially as musiciains. For example, women were almost entirely absent from the calypso tents (Chapter 3) during much of the twentieth century. By the 1930s the Carnival Queen competition, essentially a beauty pageant for light-skinned upper-class girls, established a new ideal of feminine participation in carnival. Famous nineteenth-century *jamettes*, such as Bodicea and Piti Belle Lily had no counterparts in official carnival competitions of the mid-twentieth century.

During the independence movement of the 1940s and 1950s, carnival competitions became a way to promote the agendas of cultural nationalists (e.g., see the discussion of Panorama in Chapter 5). Formal competitions still are used to promote art forms that represent certain communities of interest—such as the Soca Chutney competition, which gives Indo-Trinidadians a voice in the carnival scene, or the Pan Kaiso competition, which encourages calypsonians to write music for steelbands. To this day, competition is pervasive in carnival, both as an expression of rivalry between different neighborhoods, bands, and individuals and as a tool for promotion and control. Carnival competitions also remain embroiled in controversies about commercialization and about whether they encourage or exclude genuine artistic expression.

MUSIC

In this book I focus on carnival music genres such as calypso, steelband, and soca. Many different kinds of music, however, for many different occasions, can be heard in Trinidad; together they constitute the diverse soundscapes and aesthetic experiences that carnival music has drawn upon over the years. In the realm of what we might call "art music," for example, many Trinidadians, especially young women, take private lessons on piano and violin. Some Trinidadian men get their formal music training through service in the police or regiment (army) bands. While there is no symphony orchestra in Trinidad, opportunities exist for chamber music performance, and occasionally concerts draw larger groups together. Some people sing in choirs, such as the Lydian Singers, who perform a broad repertoire of European art music and sometimes even stage operas. Training in Indian classical music is also available, both for vocal music and for instruments such as the sitar.

Some of the institutions or events that foster musical training and performance are religious, and we may think of the associated musical genres as "religious music." Many Indo-Trinidadians learn to sing devotional songs called *bhajans* in Hindu temples and homes. At Christmastime Trinidadians love to perform and listen to *parang* music (from the Spanish word *parranda*, referring to a Christmas tradition of going from house to house singing), religious songs sung in Spanish and accompanied with guitar, cuatro, and maracas. Catholics hear chants and other types of music at mass, and Anglicans and Presbyterians sing hymns from published hymnals in their church services. Spiritual Baptists (also known as Shouters) engage in a less literate and more physically energetic music-making, spicing hymns with vocal improvisation, clapping and stamping of feet, and percussive breathing called "doptions," which generate a spiritual connection between worshipers and the Holy Spirit. Spirit possession, or "manifestation," is also the goal of music-making in the feasts of the Orisha religion (sometimes referred to in Trinidad as Shango—the name of one particular Orisha or god), which was brought to Trinidad by Yoruban people from the area of Africa that is now Nigeria. Orisha devotees practice drumming, dance, and singing that exhibit a deep connection to African musical traditions as well as certain kinds of new syncretisms and innovations (Figure 1.6; CD track 2).

FIGURE 1.6 *Orisha drums, from left to right: Oumele, which keeps a high-pitched counterrhythm; Bow, which keeps a steady bass pattern; Congo (or cutter), which improves and leads the ensemble (Rawle Gibbons).*

Many other types of music could be classified broadly as "folk music." Indo-Trinidadians perform Indian folk songs that are associated with weddings and a variety of other festive occasions, often accompanied by Indian instruments such as the *dholak* and harmonium (Figure 1.7). One of the most visible Indian folk instruments in Trinidad is the tassa drum (Figure 1.8; CD track 3), which originally was associated with the festival of Hosay (a Shiite Muslim festival known internationally as Muharram) but also has become a secular cultural symbol for Indo-Trinidadians generally, both Muslim and Hindu, and is especially popular at weddings. Tassa drumming is performed in an ensemble consisting of a large barrel-shaped drum called the *dhol* that plays a fixed pattern (Figure 1.9), a pair of brass cymbals called *jhanjh*, and the kettle-shaped tassa drum. The *dhol* player must know a variety of fixed patterns, or "hands," while the tassa player improvises within the different hands and signals changes to new hands. Tassa players often alternate with one another in a competitive and exciting display of skill that is ideally suited to festive contexts.

Many creoles have also learned to play tassa, especially in the racially mixed neighborhood of St. James in Port of Spain, where the Hosay fes-

FIGURE 1.7 *Drupatee Ramgoonai sings chutney accompanied by the "traditional" instrumentation of harmonium (a bellows-driven keyboard),* dholak *drum, and* dhantal *(a metal rod struck with a metal beater, similar in sound to a triangle). (Greg Dietrich.)*

FIGURE 1.8   *A tassa player at the Borough Day celebration in Point Fortin, accompanied by another member of his group playing* jhanjh *(cymbals).*

tival is enjoyed not only as a religious observance by devout Muslims, but also as a secular diversion for many non-Muslims. The creolization of tassa drumming is evident in the names for some of the hands, such as "dingolay" and in some musicians' reference to the tassa drum by the term "cutter," a name that also is used to describe the improvising lead drum in a variety Afro-Caribbean drum ensembles. At the same time, steelbands have sometimes incorporated tassa drums into their rhythm sections and have used tassa rhythms in their arrangements, so that tassa drumming also may be seen to represent an Indianization of creole culture.

FIGURE 1.9 *A line of* dhol *drums, played by both Indians and Creoles, accompanying tassa drums at the Hosay festival in St. James.*

European traditions also have had an important impact on Trinidadian folk music, as in the case of the quadrille, derived from the set dances of the European aristocracy and disseminated in many forms throughout the Americas during the nineteenth century. In Trinidad, as in other Caribbean islands, the different "figures" of these dance tunes were played by poor blacks in ensembles of drums and fiddles, banjos, flutes, or guitars for social dancing and even at festivals like carnival. The quadrille is no longer a significant living tradition in Trinidad, but its legacies of melody and form are expressed in calypso and other genres. African drum dances are another important genre of folk music. The Belair, or *bélé*, which features intricate coordination between dancer (usually a woman) and drummer, was brought to Trinidad by slaves from Martinique and now survives mainly in the repertoire of folk dance groups. The *bongo* is a dance done by men, especially at wakes, that is still performed in rural areas of Trinidad. The *bongo* may be accompanied by drums or by an ensemble of bamboo stamping tubes called *tamboo bamboo* (Figure 1.10).

FIGURE 1.10 Tamboo bamboo *band parading in Port of Spain as part of the Ole Mas' (old-fashioned masquerade) festivities.*

One folk performance tradition that came to be strongly identified with carnival in the nineteenth century was *kalenda* (Figure 1.11), the style of stick-fighting accompanied by song that was mentioned earlier in connection with the Canboulay Riot. The musical leader of a *kalenda* band was the *chantwell* (also spelled *chantuelle*), who composed and improvised songs that strengthened the stick-fighter when rival bands confronted one another. The *chantwell* was supported by a chorus of singers and drumming. Calypsonians of the twentieth century have their roots in this tradition of boasting and rivalry between carnival bands, as will be seen in Chapter 2.

Some genres of carnival music, such as calypso and soca, might be called "popular music," since they are disseminated commercially on radio and recordings. But the line between popular and folk, or even between popular and classical or religious music, is not always easy to draw in carnival. Soca and other genres that are marketed in recorded form (see Chapter 6) are still tied to the seasonal schedule and to the specific performance contexts of Trinidadian carnival. Also, carnival music has consistently incorporated influences from musical genres and

FIGURE 1.11 *A* kalenda *stick-fighter wards off his opponent's blow as musicians at the edge of the ring drum and sing.*

ensembles that are associated with very different performance contexts outside of carnival, as seen in the use of tassa rhythms by steelbands. The polyrhythmic drumming and call-and-response singing of *kalenda* stick-fighting music, to cite other examples, are related both to religious Orisha drumming and to secular drum dances like the *bélé* and *bongo*. When *kalenda* drums were banned following the 1881 Canboulay Riot, they were replaced by *tamboo bamboo*, and *tamboo bamboo* was the basis for the first steelbands that developed in the late 1930s (Activity 1.1; CD track 4).

ACTIVITY 1.1: LISTENING: *TAMBOO BAMBOO Your recording of* tamboo bamboo *(CD track 4) exhibits some of the traits of the common people's carnival and festival music throughout the Caribbean:*

1. It is inexpensive.
2. It is loud.
3. It is good for dancing.
4. It is inclusive, providing people of different abilities to participate as percussionists, song leaders, chorus singers, and dancers.
5. It is cyclical and improvisatory, with the song leader regulating the emotional pitch and intensity of the music.

The alternation that you hear in this recording between a soloist improvising and a chorus singing a repeated refrain is called call and response. *Musicologists refer to call and response as a "cyclical" form because the refrain (response) is constantly repeated at short intervals. Common in much West African music, call-and-response form is conducive to participation by many people, blurring the boundary between performer and audience, musician and listener. While this kind of singing tends to include many people at once, lending itself especially well to communal celebrations such as carnival, the song leader must be a skilled performer. He or she must improvise words and melody and maintain the energy and variety of the music to suit the audiences and the spaces through which the band moves.*

While *kalenda* and *tamboo bamboo* represent the African end of the carnival music spectrum, other carnival genres draw more from European traditions. I already have mentioned the importance of the quadrille in folk musical practice. Another upper-class genre that filtered into carnival folk tradition was the Venezuelan string band, featuring guitars, cuatro, violins, and sometimes piano, which became the music of choice for society dances in Trinidadian carnival around 1900. These bands were influential in calypso music, both in terms of instrumentation and melody. Brass bands comprising formally trained musicians also played an important role in carnival throughout the twentieth century. And the steelbands combine an incredible range of musical influences in their carnival music, from *tamboo bamboo* to the symphony orchestra (see Chapters 4 and 5).

Finally, different kinds of carnival music have evolved in connection with particular masquerade, dancing, or entertainment functions. *Kalenda* songs, for example, must strengthen the heart of the stick-fighter and intimidate his opponent. Blue devils, or *djab-djabs*, move their feet together in short rhythmic jumps and lunge at the crowd to the accompaniment of a raucous rhythm beat out on empty kerosene tins. Black-faced minstrels sing folk and minstrel songs from the United States, accompanied by banjo. Calypsonians performing for seated audiences tell stories and jokes in long, slow ballads. On carnival Monday, masqueraders want hot soca music to "wine their waist," "get on bad," and show off their beautiful costumes and bodies. But by Tuesday night, a steelband may move whole neighborhoods of tired masqueraders across town to their homes with a sweet, slow calypso. The most popular and well-known kinds of carnival music that we focus on here are part of this complex whole of Trinidadian performance traditions.

CHAPTER 2

The Man of Words

∞

Although the name "calypso" probably was coined in Trinidad, the roots of this music lie in African song as well as in European folk traditions such as ballads, a combined heritage that manifests itself throughout the Caribbean. Calypso is performed at seasonal celebrations in the English-speaking islands, such as Carnival in Trinidad, Crop Over in Barbados, or Junkanoo in the Bahamas. With the advent of the recording industry in the early twentieth century, calypso also became a mediated "popular music," and the Trinidadian version gained particular fame and influence in the Caribbean and internationally. Calypsonians from Trinidad made recordings in New York as early as 1912, and in 1914 Victor sent a recording expedition to the island. Decca and Sony later recorded many calypsonians as well. Trinidadian calypso enjoyed significant commercial success in the United States from the 1930s through 1950s, which, along with the entepreneurship of local record producers and distributors, boosted distribution of Trinidadian music throughout the English Caribbean. Today, despite the vitality of several other local calypso traditions, Trinidadian carnival is generally recognized as the hub of the art form.

Because the appreciation of text and language is fundamental to calypso, the calypsonian is a good example of what folklorist Roger Abrahams calls the "Man of Words," a broad performance tradition in the West Indies, and African American culture generally, that stresses both verbal dueling and elegant formal speaking. According to one theory, the very word "calypso" is rooted in an appreciation for verbal dexterity: the term is thought to be an anglicized version of "kaiso," a word that may derive from the Hausa language in Africa and that is still used by Trinidadians to express their pleasure at a clever turn of words in a calypso performance. Because Trinidadians prize the verbal tradition of calypso so highly, I have chosen to begin with a focus on calypso texts, leaving more detailed discussion of their musical setting for Chapter 3.

FROM *CHANTWELL* TO CALYPSONIAN

Modern calypso in Trinidad is related to the functions of the nineteenth-century *chantwell* and the contrasting contexts of the road and the tent. The first calypsonians were, in fact, *chantwells* (carnival band song leaders) who around 1900 began to perform in temporary carnival season structures for audiences who were eager to hear a preview of the new carnival songs. Since as early as 1921, when Chieftain Douglas contracted with a group of *chantwells* to perform for middle-class Trinidadians in his Railroad Millionaires calypso tent, this practice has been a formal entertainment business. Douglas catered to people who were interested in the public carnival and its music but preferred to listen to the *chantwells'* songs in a controlled and safe environment. One of the first singers to make the transition from *chantwell* to calypsonian was a middle-class jacket man named Julian Whiterose, whose calypso name was the Iron Duke and who was himself a stick-fighter and a *chantwell*. His 1914 song, "Iron Duke in the Land" (CD track 5), the first calypso to be recorded in Trinidad, is spiced with the patois argot of the stick-fighter, as well as grandiloquent English that proclaims him to be both a fighter and a formidable man of words. The words of the second verse, chorus, and third verse are as follows:

> *At my appearance upon the scene*
> *Julius the devil played the Cord*
> *And still I am the head of fraternal order*
> *Calling, sweeping to all the agony*
> *Achieving my surprising majesty*
> *In blending, beaming, and swaying*
> *Jumping this way, bawling, "Clear de way, Whiterose joli*
> *Djable re-re-o" [Handsome Whiterose, the devil king]*

(Chorus:)

> *Iron Duke in the land*
> *Fire brigade*
> *Iron Duke in the land*
> *Fire brigade*
> *Bring the locomotive*
> *Just because it's a fire federation*
> *Bring the locomotive*
> *Just because it's a fire federation*
> *Sans humanité*

It was a modern manifestation
Of the elder civilization
That muh carnival celebration
Of this social organization
It called to mind to an abstention
Over all the population
I, Julian, taking the social décor, deh who whey, Whiterose Union
Sans humanité

In the early days of the tents, confrontations between calypsonians were staged in song duels called *picong*. The term "picong" also refers more broadly to derision and insults, including those traded between calypsonians, whether or not they share the same stage (examples of both song duel and indirect picong, between the Mighty Sparrow and Lord Melody, can be heard on Rounder's *Calypso Awakening* album). Whether or not songs were about fighting and confrontation, it remained common practice throughout the 1920s and into the 1930s to sing the refrain "sans humanité" (without pity) at the end of calypso verses, a convention that probably derives from *kalenda* stick-fighting songs.

In addition to their role in interband conflicts, *chantwells* were entertainers, and their jokes, obscenities, and spicy commentaries on the political and social scandals of the day delighted the crowds. Carnival revelers responded to and encouraged the *chantwell's* improvisations by singing along at the chorus. With the advent of the calypso tents (Chapter 3), these choral refrains and improvisations became the basis for more elaborate and lengthy compositions. Some of the different themes and styles of calypso—for example, social and political commentary, boasting, humor, smut (obscene calypsoes), nation-building, and road march—will be illustrated here in the works of a few modern calypsonians.

THE LORD KITCHENER

One important category of calypso is the road march, a song for dancing in the street on carnival day. Words are important for a good road march, since the public likes to sing along while dancing, but this type of calypso is judged as much by its rhythms and melodies as its text. A calypsonian whose music set the standard for the road march during the 1940s through the 1970s was the Lord Kitchener (Aldwyn Roberts). One of the few modern calypsonians who actually got his start singing as a carnival *chantwell*, Kitchener began performing in his home town of Arima in the 1930s (Figure 2.1). Kitchener, whose prodigious career spanned the six decades before his death in 2000 and who was affectionately known as the "Grandmaster," was especially popular with the steelbands because his music made people want to dance and sing along even in instrumental rendition. Kitchener's contributions to calypso are broad, but I will postpone further discussion of his music until Chapter 5, where I focus on the way he composed for the steelband.

THE MIGHTY SPARROW

Many Trinidadians argue that the Mighty Sparrow (Slinger Francisco) is the greatest calypsonian of all time (the Lord Kitchener being the other favorite for this honor). The Mighty Sparrow began his career in 1954 and, although he has withdrawn from the tents and from competition, he was still performing at the time of this book's writing. His songs span the gamut of calypso themes, from smut to politics, usually combining serious commentary with humor. Even his stage name is an ironic

FIGURE 2.1 *The Lord Kitchener (Aldwyn Roberts), dressed in the hat and suit favored by early twentieth-century calypsonians. CD cover from ICE 941802, 1994.*

commentary on the tendency of his contemporaries to choose intimidating sobriquets. His choice of the name "Mighty Sparrow" suggests that the speed and wit of a little bird can prevail over a Roaring Lion, a Lord Kitchener, an Atilla the Hun, or a Mighty Bomber. Unlike most calypsonians, Sparrow is known for his rich and nuanced singing voice, and has recorded many ballads as well as calypsoes. Sparrow is also a charismatic performer, dancing and teasing with impeccable timing as he tells his stories (Figure 2.2).

The song "Jean and Dinah" (CD track 6) won both the Calypso King and the Road March titles in 1956, an extraordinary feat that cemented Sparrow's reputation as a new star. The Calypso King competition (or Calypso Monarch competition, as it later became titled to include female calypsonians) is based on performances for seated audiences in the calypso tents, while the Road March is the most popular tune for dancing on carnival day (Chapter 3). Although it is extremely rare for the same song to be the favorite on the road and in the tents, most good calypsoes combine danceability and fun with a message of some kind. "Jean and Dinah" is energetic and fun for the road, but at the same time its lyrics say something important about social experience and history.

FIGURE 2.2 *The Mighty Sparrow (Slinger Francisco). CD cover from ICE 921002, 1992.*

At the time Sparrow wrote the song, the U.S. Navy had withdrawn many of its troops from its base in Trinidad, established with England's consent during World War II (the base was finally closed in 1967). Sparrow uses the distress of prostitutes in Port of Spain as a metaphor for the fears many Trinidadians had about the economic losses that would result from the departure of U.S. armed forces. The characterization of the losers in this development as prostitutes pokes fun at such economic fears, depicting Trinidad's relationship to the Americans as a greedy sellout.

Well the girls in town feeling bad
No more Yankees in Trinidad
They gonna close down the base for good
Them girls have to make out how they could
Brother is now they park up in town
In for a penny, and in for a pound
Believe me it's competition for so
Trouble in town when the price drop low.

The tone of the chorus is celebratory, as Sparrow mocks the prostitutes pitilessly and proclaims the restoration of his own authority (and, by extension, Trinidad's control over its own affairs). On carnival day in 1956, thousands of Trinidadians exuberantly endorsed these sentiments as they sang Sparrow's bouncy chorus in the streets (as you can hear at the end of the steelband rendition of "Jean and Dinah" in CD track 7):

Jean and Dinah
Rosita and Clementina, round the corner posing
Bet your life is something they selling
And if you catch them broke, you can get them all for nothing
Don't make no row
The Yankees gone, Sparrow take over now

It is difficult to characterize "Jean and Dinah" as just one type of calypso, since the song combines social and political commentary with humor and smut, all set to an engaging and danceable melody. The ability to entertain and educate simultaneously has been characteristic of the Mighty Sparrow's style and career.

THE MIGHTY CHALKDUST

In contrast to the Mighty Sparrow, the Mighty Chalkdust (Hollis Liverpool) is known as a calypsonian who specializes in one type of calypso, political commentary. This is not to say that Chalkdust is not versatile; he delivers his messages with plenty of humor and sexual double entendre, too. Chalkdust initially made his reputation, however, as a critic of the government during the 1970s, when Trinidad was experiencing the social upheaval of the Black Power movement and the economic turbulence of the oil industry's boom and bust. These events contributed to a sober reassessment of Trinidad's progress after the euphoria of independence and provoked extensive political commentary from calypsonians. Although he is not known for his road marches, Chalkdust has been highly successful in the tent, winning the Calypso Monarch title five times between 1976 and 1993 (Figure 2.3).

FIGURE 2.3 *The Mighty Chalkdust (Hollis Liverpool). Album cover from* Total Kaiso, *Straker's GS 2298.*

The sobriquet "Chalkdust" refers to Liverpool's profession as a schoolteacher. The pursuit of a nonmusic profession is typical for most calypsonians, because singing is seasonal work in Trinidad, and (with the exception of a few stars like Mighty Sparrow, Lord Kitchener, and David Rudder) few calypsonians can get enough work abroad to make a living outside the carnival season. Chalkdust strengthened his intellectual credentials when he completed a Ph.D. in history and ethnomusicology at the University of Michigan in 1993. This is an unusual accomplishment among calypsonians, who have traditionally been regarded as common people who just happen to have a sort of "native wit" and understanding of history, society, and politics. There have been other educated middle-class calypsonians over the years, though, including jacket men like Julian Whiterose and Atilla the Hun (Raymond Quevedo), who served on the Port of Spain City Council and on Trinidad's colonial Legislative Council during the 1940s and 1950s.

Chalkdust's 1989 song, "Chauffeur Wanted" (CD track 8) which won him the Calypso Monarch title, is an attack on the government of the National Alliance for Reconciliation (NAR), which had recently dealt an election defeat to the PNM, (inextricably associated with the charismatic Prime Minister Eric Williams until his death in 1982) for the first time since Trinidad's independence in 1962. Chalkdust uses the metaphor of a maxi-taxi (a sort of minivan bus or taxi) with a bad driver to criticize the new prime minister, A. N. R. Robinson, in particular:

You asking me what is wrong with Trinidad
You can't understand why things gone so bad
You find we so rich in human resources
And yet the country going to pieces
Well let me tell you my friend where we went wrong
After Eric Williams old car break down
We called in NAR, we ordered a next car
And installed a new driver

With thirty-three passengers from the party
We gave him a maxi-taxi
Fitted with mag wheels, tape deck, computer
Air conditioned, eight cylinder
With posh new fittings this maxi-car arrive
Then it start to swerve and nose dive
It took a year for passengers to realize
They say, "The new driver cannot drive"

Notice that the target of Chalkdust's critique is never named, but simply is referred to as the "driver." It is a common convention in calypso to avoid naming the target of one's derision and satire explicitly, a convention Chalkdust himself calls the "mask" of the calypsonian. This form of etiquette has a precedent in West African tradition and was reinforced during slavery, when songs were used to convey secret messages that the masters could not understand. The cloaking of sexual references in double entendre (Preacher's song about "fruit," for example, in Chapter 1) is another expression of this principle. Because calypso uses so much metaphor and double entendre, much of which refers to local people and events, it is often difficult for non-Trinidadians to understand everything that is being conveyed; early in the history of calypso the same could have been said of upper-class Trinidadians who were unfamiliar with lower-class speech idioms. While Chalkdust's driver metaphor is relatively obvious, others are more subtle, and calypsonians even delight in seeing people enjoy their music when they don't really understand what is being said.

DAVID RUDDER

David Rudder burst onto the calypso scene unexpectedly in 1986 when he became Calypso Monarch in the same year that he won the Young Kings, a junior calypso competition. Since then he has not won the Calypso Monarch title again, partly because of questions about whether his music can properly be considered calypso. Even his decision to perform under his own name instead of adopting a calypso sobriquet offended some purists. While his innovative experiments with calypso have caused him problems with the Calypso Monarch judges (he no longer participates in the competition), they have inspired many fans both in Trinidad and abroad, and Rudder has become the most successful recording artist in Trinidad. Rudder has said that he is true to what is most important about calypso, speaking to the experience and concerns of the people, but he does not feel bound to abide by all of calypso's rules and conventions. Unlike most calypsonians, David Rudder over the years has worked fairly consistently with the same band, known originally as Charlie's Roots. Together they have written songs and arrangements that draw on Trinidadian folk music; on Spiritual Baptist and Orisha religious music; on Caribbean and Latin styles such as reggae, salsa, and samba; and on U.S. rhythm and blues, soul, and gospel. Rudder has a reputation as an intellectual and a visionary; he writes songs that call attention to problems as well as songs that celebrate the beauty and goodness of Trinidadians and Caribbean people generally (Figure 2.4).

David Rudder's 1998 song, "High Mas'" (CD track 9), is an example of the latter; it also might fall into the category of a "nation-building" calypso (although it is not as overtly patriotic or political as many calypsoes of this type). The title of "High Mas'" plays on the Trinidadian word for "masquerade," casting the bacchanal of carnival as a spiritual experience akin to the Catholic high mass. This analogy challenges a view that dates from the English colonial period, and that is still held by many people in Trinidad, that carnival—in particular the kind of sexual license that people take in carnival dancing—is essentially immoral. Instead the song implies that music, "wining" (a kind of dancing that involves winding the waist and pelvis) and "having a good time" (including "liming," or socializing/partying with friends) are spiritually healing. The lyrics of the verse are suggestive of the Christian Lord's Prayer ("Our Father who art in heaven") and are sung in a monotone

FIGURE 2.4 *David Rudder. CD cover of* Beloved, *Lypsoland CR 028.*

that invokes the style of plain chant used in Anglican or Catholic church services.

Our Father who has given us this art
So that we can all feel like we are a part
Of this earthly heaven
Amen
Forgive us this day our daily weaknesses
As we seek to cast our mortal burdens on this city
Amen
Oh merciful father, in this bacchanal season where men lose their reason
But most of us just want to wine and have a good time cause we looking
 for a lime
Because we feeling fine, Lord
Amen
And as we jump up and down in this crazy town
Send us some music for some healing
Amen

The chorus is more melodically energetic and invites listeners to participate, both by joining in the call-and-response singing and by putting up their hands. Similar instructions to the dancers can be heard in many contemporary carnival songs (such as Superblue's "Pump It Up," described at the beginning of Chapter 1). However, the exhortation here to "give praise" and the invocation of Jah (the Rastafarian name for God) also evoke the common use of this gesture in charismatic Christian worship services.

Everybody hand raise
Everybody give praise
Everybody hand raise
And if you know what I mean...
Put up your finger
And if you know what I mean...
Put up your hand
And if you know what I mean...
Put up your finger
And if you know what I mean then scream
Oooh! Give Jah his praises

While its melody might not be jumpy enough for a steelband on *j'ouvert* morning, "High Mas'" is a calypso that is thought-provoking (in a more intellectual and serious way than "Jean and Dinah") and dance-provoking at the same time.

SINGING SANDRA

One of the most powerful voices of social conscience to emerge in calypso during recent years is that of Singing Sandra (Sandra Des Vignes). Sandra began in the tents in 1984 and gained wider attention when she began to sing with three other women (Lady B, Marvelous Marva, and Tigress) as the United Sisters in 1991. This was an unusual strategy for calypsonians, who almost always perform and promote themselves as individuals (to even have a regular band, as David Rudder does, is fairly unusual). The United Sisters who had a big hit in 1993 with the song "Whoa Donkey," projected a powerful and confident female identity in a profession that is notoriously sexist. In 1999 Singing Sandra, performing by herself again, was crowned Calypso Monarch, the only woman since Calypso Rose (who won in 1978) to win the title (Figure 2.5).

Sandra's moralizing stance and emotionally intense performance reflect her upbringing in the Spiritual Baptist church, and her solo calypsoes have been of the social commentary variety, stressing issues such as economic injustice and gender inequality. Her winning song in 1999, "Voices," drew attention to the misery and frustrations of Trinidad's urban poor. In 2000 she sang about the problem of fathers who don't raise their children in "Caribbean Man Part 2" (CD track 10):

> *Two adults in the home but only one parent*
> *Well this is the modern Caribbean scene*
> *Go to any PTA meeting or any school sports day*
> *And you gon' see exactly what I mean*
> *Caribbean man you abdicate your throne*
> *The task of rearing children falling on woman alone*
> *So the youths embracing crime and it getting worse*
> *There's only one way for this to reverse—Hear me!*

> *Your duty you must affirm,*
> *Man contribute more than sperm*
> *Our young sons you got to shape*
> *So they won't abuse and rape*
> *The youths today they getting a fright; too much deadbeat fathers and that*
> * ain't right*

FIGURE 2.5 *Singing Sandra (Sandra Des Vignes) at the 2000 Calypso Monarch Finals, dressed in an elegant version of the Spiritual Baptists' traditional white dress and turban.*

Instead of romping in the bedroom, your headship role you got to resume
Caribbean man
Instead of looking 'bout for romance, pull up your zip, time to wear the
    pants
Caribbean man

This song plays on the title of Black Stalin's 1979 song "Caribbean Man," in which he called for unity between people who shared the same African heritage and the same history of slavery and social struggle. Sandra's reference to that message does not diminish the importance of racial pride or solidarity, but it questions whether this goal can be achieved without justice between the sexes, or within families. Sandra thus engages in a sort of time-lapse picong with Stalin, but her message is aimed more broadly at the complacent sexism about which most contemporary male calypsonians choose not to sing. While calypso throughout the twenthieth century has clearly been a *Man* of Words tradition, Sandra's success and her uncompromising conscience are helping to make a place for more women's voices. Indeed, another woman, Denyse Plummer, opened the twenty-first century by winning the 2001 Calypso Monarch title.

⮑

I have chosen to introduce calypso through a discussion of words and texts because this is the aspect of calypso that is most frequently cited as its distinguishing feature. In performance, of course, calypso texts are rendered in melody and accompanied by musical instruments. Sometimes calypsoes are even performed without words, as in the renditions by steelbands. Calypso must also be understood, therefore, as a genre that is characterized by particular conventions of melody, harmony, rhythm, form, instrumentation, and so on that constitute a *musical style*. The next chapter describes calypso musical style in relation to its main performance contexts.

CHAPTER 3

Calypso in the Tent and on the Road

∞

During the weeks preceding carnival, calypsonians perform in several theaters or auditoriums in Port of Spain, permanent structures that are referred to as calypso "tents." The term dates from the 1910s, when calypso began to be sung in temporary structures erected for carnival. Performing in a tent before seated audiences, singers tend to focus on storytelling and word play, and it is here that calypso's verbal tradition has its greatest scope. But some of the songs performed in the tent are also popular for dancing to at fetes and on carnival day. Calypso, therefore, is also dance music, and, despite the diversity of themes in calypso lyrics, its dance function is the basis for a certain consistency in the musical setting. This chapter briefly reviews the performance contexts of calypso, and then discusses aspects of calypso musical style as they relate to its dual functions of storytelling and dance.

THE TENT

Calypso tents open soon after New Year and stage nightly performances all the way up until carnival. The most popular tents in Port of Spain include Spektakula, Calypso Review, and Kaiso House, each of which has exclusive performing contracts with fifteen to twenty calypsonians (calypsonians thus do not perform in more than one tent, although they may still record and perform at fetes and concerts elsewhere). To draw an audience, a tent must have a number of popular veterans in its stable, but tents also recruit new talent—singers who become known through junior calypso competitions or acquire a reputation performing at fetes. An evening's performance consists of a dozen or more calypsonians singing one at a time. The less well-known artists tend to perform early in the evening, while the big names sing at or near the end so the audience won't leave early.

Although every tent has its own unique physical layout, each of them features a raised stage from which singers look out toward a seated audience. The calypsonian is alone at the front of the stage with a hand-held microphone, pacing or sometimes dancing to and fro, while a chorus (usually of three female singers, but sometimes including a man) stands to one side, singing intermittently and swaying to the music with elegant coordinated movements. At the rear of the stage sits the house band—typically consisting of electric keyboard, guitar, bass, drumset, percussion, saxophones, and trumpets—which accompanies every singer. A master of ceremonies (who is as important as the calypsonians to a tent's success) introduces each singer and tells jokes between appearances.

Each calypsonian performs two songs during his or her turn on stage. Often one of these songs has a more serious tone, dealing with social issues, political controversies, or national pride, and the other song is more light-hearted and festive. This formula is repeated at the annual Calypso Monarch competition, in which the winning calypsonian is awarded a new car, a substantial cash prize, and a great deal of prestige. The Calypso Monarch competition acknowledges calypso's role as a music of festivity and dancing, which is one reason calypsonians often include one "up-tempo" song in their tent repertoire, but the judges tend to give more weight to more slow-paced narrative "message" calypsoes. Some calypsonians who specialize in particular types of songs, such as humor or political satire, may depart from this formula to exercise their own strengths and preferences.

The audience in the tent enjoys the music, and people may occasionally even stand up and dance, but the atmosphere in the calypso tent is characterized by careful attention to the words and their delivery. Audience members regularly shout their approval at a clever double entendre (a disguised sexual reference), a funny story, a political criticism, or a humorous imitation of another calypsonian or a public figure. A calypsonian whose song is applauded enthusiastically will come back to sing an extra verse. A few singers can improvise these new verses on the spot, while others must compose an extra verse or two for encores. As the season progresses they often compose more verses for a successful song. Calypsonians sometimes respond to and challenge one another in song, and audiences particularly enjoy this kind of picong, although it is rarely done today between two performers sharing the same stage.

Calypsonians singing in the tent cultivate a distinctive stage persona through their choice of a calypso name, the style of songs they sing, and the way they dress. The Shadow (Winston Bailey) always wears somber black clothing to match the carnival theme of death and mystery that his name conveys (Figure 3.1). Singing Sandra wears elaborate head wraps and gowns that reflect her Spiritual Baptist faith (Figure 2.5). The Mighty Chalkdust wears elegant and colorful shirt jackets that may be seen as modern manifestations of the African heritage he often points to in his songs. Denyse Plummer often sings songs about carnival festivity and spirit, and her costumes reflect the extravagant and dazzling styles of modern carnival masqueraders (Figure 3.2).

THE ROAD

While costumes, gestures, and sometimes even brief skits add flavor to the calypsonian's storytelling on stage, these dramatic embellishments are possible only on the stage of the calypso tent. For the road on car-

FIGURE 3.1   *The Shadow (Winston Bailey) at the 2000 Calypso Monarch Finals, dressed as usual in black.*

FIGURE 3.2 *Denyse Plummer at the 2000 Calypso Monarch Finals, evoking the spirit of fancy mas' with a glittering costume.*

nival day, the drama is left to the masqueraders. Songs must stand on their own, either in recorded versions or in steelband renditions. The expectations of dancing masqueraders on the road differ in important ways from those of seated audiences in the tents, and this difference in context corresponds to a somewhat different musical style in calypsoes that are intended as "road marches."

On carnival Monday and Tuesday, the streets of Port of Spain are criss-crossed by masquerade bands. Some are small neighborhood bands with homemade costumes, while others have thousands of members who are grouped in sections, each with matching costumes that form a shifting spectacle of beautiful colors and shapes as they pass. Big or small, every masquerade band has music. Music sets the pace at

which the masqueraders move, gives them the energy to "play mas'"
and dance for hours, and regulates their movements and moods, as fren-
zies of excitement and energy alternate with more relaxing grooves. In
Port of Spain today most masquerade bands hire one or more DJ trucks,
flatbeds loaded with massive speakers that blare recorded music. Some
trucks also carry live bands featuring popular calypsonians and soca
singers. In the 1950s and 1960s, steelbands were the music of choice for
the road, and calypsonians depended on the steelbands to popularize
their songs (in instrumental renditions) on carnival day. Whatever the
format—live or recorded, instrumental or vocal—music for the road has
always been essential to carnival, and it has been the job of the *chantwell*
and the calypsonian to supply it.

Compared to calypsoes for the tent, songs for the road are generally
faster in tempo, have catchier and more singable melodies (often featuring call and response at the chorus), have a more energetic rhythm,
and use exciting breaks to stimulate the dancers. These differences form
part of the distinction between calypso and the more recent genre of
soca, which is the favorite music today for the carnival road and at fetes
(Chapter 6). But the line between calypso and soca is sometimes blurry,
in part because calypso has a long history as dance music. Indeed, the
distinction between road march and tent calypso dates at least to the
1910s, when *chantwells* first came off the street to perform in tents.

Each year the Road March title is granted to the singer whose song
is played (live or recorded) the most times by masquerade bands as they
pass the judging points. On a few rare occasions the same song has won
both Road March and Calypso Monarch honors (e.g., Mighty Sparrow's
"Jean and Dinah" in 1956, David Rudder's "Bahia Girl" in 1986). Many
calypsonians, however, have won Road March and Calypso Monarch
title in different years, which further underscores the important relationship between music for the road and music for the tent. It is plau-
sible, therefore, to discuss calypso musical style in terms of certain elements that are normative both for the tent and for the road, provided
that one is attentive to how these elements vary in different performance
contexts and in different historical periods. I have chosen here to discuss instrumentation, form, rhythmic feel, phrasing, and breaks.

INSTRUMENTATION

One of the largest differences between calypso recordings from different eras is the instruments accompanying the singer. Although singers
in the tents today are accompanied by a large band with brass and electric instruments, most calypsonians also can sing while accompanying

themselves on guitar, and they occasionally perform this way in intimate contexts. A calypsonian typically crafts a melody and chord progression that will work well with simple guitar accompaniment, so calypsoes tend to be less dependent than some other genres of song (such as reggae, rock and roll, or rap) on a specific instrumentation, arrangement, or studio production.

In CD track 5, "Iron Duke in the Land" sung by Julien Whiterose in 1914, the accompanying instruments are guitar and cuatro (Figure 3.3). The guitar picks out a sort of melodic baseline. The cuatro, a four-string guitar-type instrument from Venezuela, strums the changing chords in a consistent rhythmic pattern. These instruments were popularized in

FIGURE 3.3 *The conventional six-string Spanish guitar (right) and the small four-string Venezuelan cuatro.*

carnival by nineteenth-century Venezuelan-style string bands that also included violins, upright bass, and piano. The cuatro, in particular, became a favorite instrument for calypso because of its piercing sound and driving rhythmic energy. The use of a rhythmic strum has remained fundamental to calypso style, whether played on a cuatro, a guitar, an electric guitar, a steel pan, or an electronic keyboard (see Activity 3.1).

ACTIVITY 3.1: LISTENING—CUATRO VERSUS GUITAR IN "IRON DUKE IN THE LAND" *Try to distinguish the guitar from the cuatro as you listen to "Iron Duke in the Land" CD track 5. The cuatro plays chords (several notes together) in a regular rhythmic strum, while the guitar plucks single, lower-pitched notes that are constantly changing (basically the guitar is playing a bass line).*

From the 1920s through the 1940s many calypso recordings featured a jazz style instrumental accompaniment, sometimes including banjo, upright bass, piano, trumpet, and clarinet or saxophone (many included violin as well, an influence of the Venezuelan string bands). This reflected the international popularity of jazz and also attested to the fact that calypsonians were making recordings that sold not only in Trinidad but in the United States and other countries. In fact, many of the calypso records during this time were made in New York City. The Keskidee Trio, for example, featuring three of the most popular Trinidadian calypsonians of the 1930s—Atilla the Hun, Lord Beginner, and Tiger—recorded "Congo Bara" with an introduction that almost sounds like the contemporary music of Duke Ellington (CD track 11). Because "Congo Bara" is presented as a folk song, the rest of this performance uses an older style of instrumentation, but most recordings by these same calypsonians used jazz instrumentation throughout. To this day, in fact, a brass section of trumpets and saxophones continues to be an integral part of the calypso sound, playing occasional countermelodies or answers to the singer (e.g., in the chorus of "Jean and Dinah") and often providing an instrumental rendition of the melody as an interlude between the sung verses.

By the 1950s, calypso recordings showed the influence of instrumentation in other styles of popular music, such as rhythm and blues and Cuban *son*. Mighty Sparrow's 1956 recording of "Jean and Dinah," for example, features electric guitar, drumset, and bongos. In later eras percussion instruments became increasingly prominent in calypso recordings, which is indicative not only of changing ideas about instrumentation but also of changing recording technology. The maracas, for example (or *shac shacs*, as they are called in Trinidad), which were commonly used to accompany live calypso performance in the early twentieth century, tended not to be used on records. This may have been partly because of the aesthetic preferences that prevailed in recording studios, but in the early days of electronic recording it was also difficult to record maracas without drowning out the singer. By the 1960s, however, the drumset became common on calypso recordings, and from the 1970s onward the use of cowbells, congas, and synthesized drum sounds proliferated (see Activity 3.2). The same period saw increased use of electronic instruments (bass, guitar, keyboards) and synthesized sounds. The synthesized sounds and studio production effects of some recordings played on the road today cannot be accurately reproduced by live bands in the tents (a change associated especially with soca that will be discussed further in Chapter 6).

ACTIVITY 3.2: INSTRUMENTATION IN "JEAN AND DINAH" AND "HIGH MAS'" *Compare the instrumental accompaniment in the Mighty Sparrow's 1956 song, "Jean and Dinah" (CD track 6), with David Rudder's 1998 song, "High Mas'" (CD track 9). Notice the greater variety and prominence of percussion in "High Mas'" that is characteristic of modern calypso recordings.*

FORM

The form or structure of a calypso song is related closely to the structure of its text and to its performance context. Carnival songs of the nineteenth and early twentieth centuries were called *lavways*, short refrains sung by a chorus and interspersed with the improvisations of a solo singer. As noted previously, this call-and-response format gave the *chantwell* the opportunity to lead the song and display his improvisatory skill, while at the same time encouraging participation from others who sang the chorus or played accompanying rhythms on percussion instruments. Listen, for example, to "Congo Bara," an old *lavway* that the Keskidee Trio preserved on record (Activity 3.3; CD track 11).

ACTIVITY 3.3: "CONGO BARA"   *CD track 11 is a 1935 recording by the Keskidee Trio of a famous nineteenth-century* lavway. *The words express the laments of prisoners, and the song is named after the prison guard Congo Bara. The singers take turns playing the part of song leader, singing most of their solos in French patois, the language of working-class Trinidadians in the nineteenth century. The chorus is also in patois:*

Prisonniers levé.
Mettez limié bai Congo Bara

*[Prisonners arise,
Give Congo Bara some light]*

After learning to sing the chorus in patois, try to come up with a chorus in English (or whatever language you like) that is patterned on the melody and rhythm of the "Congo Bara" chorus but relates to an interesting event at your own school, in your family, or concerning some subject that is meaningful to you. Have different people come up with solos (patterned rhythmically and melodically on the solos in the recording) that are thematically related to your chorus.

When you perform your song (accompanied by guitar and maracas if possible) you will be singing in the true calypso tradition of verbal invention and topical commentary.

Old *lavways* are sometimes incorporated into the choruses of modern calypsoes; call and response thus continues to be an important small-scale form within a larger form. The Lord Kitchener's "Pan in A Minor" (CD track track 12) uses call and response in the chorus, where the words "beat pan" are answered by changing instrumental lines. This kind of use of call and response goes over especially well on the road, where people enjoy joining in the singing of the chorus.

While calypsoes may incorporate call-and-response form in certain sections, the overall form of calypso songs is always *strophic*, meaning that several different verses or stanzas of text are set to a repeated melody. Most calypsoes also have a chorus, a recurring section of the song in which the same melody *and* text are repeated. This "verse and chorus" form parallels the *lavway*'s alternation of soloist and chorus, but on a much more extended time scale, and usually without improvisation (although a few calypsonians are still expert at improvising in rhyming verse, a practice referred to as "extempo"). Like the *lavway*, the modern calypso chorus is usually written to be catchy and singable and invites the public to participate. Both "Iron Duke in the Land" (CD track 5) and "Jean and Dinah" (CD track 6) have simple verse and chorus structures: the calypsonian sings several verses, each of which has new words, and after each verse a group of singers sings a repeated chorus.

Other calypsoes may only have one line of repeated text in each verse, which we could describe as a "refrain" rather than a chorus. The Mighty Chalkdust's "Chauffeur Wanted" is an example of this: "The new driver cannot drive" is the refrain that is sung at the end of each verse. The phrase "sans humanité," heard in "Iron Duke in the Land," was also a stock refrain used by many calypsonians. The use of a brief refrain at the end of a long verse is a convention that was established in the early 1900s, when calypsonians began singing eight-line "oratorical" calypsoes, and that continued in the narrative "ballad" calypsoes of the 1920s and 1930s that told stories for listening in the tents rather than for dancing and singing along.

Many calypsoes use standard chord progressions that also contribute to our sense of form in the music—the predictability of certain sequences of chords, that is, gives experienced listeners a sense of direction, progress, tension, and resolution. The verse of "Iron Duke in the Land" is an example of the "old minor," or "sans humanité," calypso— a standard chord progression along with which the first line of text is usually repeated (although not in this example) and each verse ends with a consistent refrain, often the formulaic "sans humanité" (see Activity 3.4). Because the old minor calypso form was so common in the 1910s through the 1930s, it is often remarked that calypso uses a limited number of stock melodies. This, of course, made text and word play all the more important.

ACTIVITY 3.4: "IRON DUKE IN THE LAND" CHORD
PROGRESSION (CD TRACK 5) *A chord is combination
of three or more notes that sound together. Each chord is
built on a "root" note that is one of the steps of the musical
scale, so chords are often described with roman numerals that
indicate the root: "I" indicates a chord built on the first step
of the scale, "V" indicates a chord built on the fifth step, and
so on. A series of chords, called a "chord progression," functions
musically to create harmonic tension, anticipation, and
resolution.*

*In this diagram the text is organized in terms of musical me-
ter. Each "/" represents the beginning of a new measure, a regularly recurring period that measures the musical time. Chord
changes occur at the beginning of a measure, following a predictable rhythm. Even if you don't really know what the roman
numeral symbols mean, try to hear the cuatro changing the chords
it strums as you listen.*

It was a . . .

modern manife-	/station	of the	/elder civili-	/zation	Thay my
i	i		V	i	
carnival cele-	/bration	of this	/social organi-	/zation	It
i	i		V	I	
called to mind an ab-	/stention	over	/all the popu-	/lation	I Julian taking the
I7	iv		VII7	III	
social décor, deh who	/whey Whiterose Union/		sans humanité		
I7	iv		V7	i	

The chorus of Mighty Sparrow's "Jean and Dinah" uses a different
chord progression in the major mode that is also common to many calypsoes (see Activity 3.5). (Jazz musicians will recognize the second half
of this chord progression as "rhythm changes" named for the George
Gershwin song "I Got Rhythm.")

ACTIVITY 3.5: "JEAN AND DINAH" CHORD PROGRESSION (CD TRACK 6) *See Activity 3.4 for an explanation of this diagram. The strum here is more difficult to hear than in "Iron Duke," so it may be easier to detect the changing chords by focusing on the bass line.*

Jean and Dinah	/Rosita and	/Clementina	/round the
I	I	V	V
corner posing	/Bet your life is	/something they sellin	/And if you
V	V	I	I
catch them broken,	/you can get them	/all for nothing	/Don't make no
I	I7	IV	iv
row, the	/yankees gone,	/Sparrow take over	/now
I	I vi	ii V	I

Since the 1960s, calypsonians have used increasingly complex verse forms and more diverse chord progressions. This has occurred partly in response to the musical needs of steelbands (Chapter 5). It also reflects the increasing exposure of calypsonians to other popular music traditions through radio and records, as well as new opportunities (exemplified by the success abroad of the Lord Kitchener and later the Mighty Sparrow) to succeed as international entertainers. Despite the increased variety of forms and chord progressions, however, calypso's basic rhythmic structure, what I will refer to here as "rhythmic feel," has remained fairly constant.

RHYTHMIC FEEL

Calypso's rhythmic character derives from its function as dance music for the road and carries over into other contexts. Like many other genres of dance music, calypso has a rhythmic quality that is distinctive and recognizable. If you are Trinidadian, your body will recognize this "rhythmic feel," and you will likely to respond to it by dancing. I attempt here to describe aspects of calypso's rhythmic feel in words; but people more commonly express their understanding of this feel by moving, dancing, and singing. Because the rhythmic feel of calypso is fundamentally connected to Trinidadian styles of dancing, you must have the experience of dancing to it to really understand calypso!

On the road at carnival time, people travel as they dance, processing down the street in costume or just tagging along behind the band in their street clothes. The main style of dancing in this context entails a simple alternation of the feet—left, right, left, right—in a swaying short-stepped kind of walk referred to as "chipping" (the name comes from the sound of leather shoe soles scraping the pavement in unison— "chip, chip, chip, chip"). Listen to the bass in the Mighty Sparrow's "Jean and Dinah" (CD track 6), and you will hear that it plays on a steady pulse, matching the pace of a dancer's evenly spaced footsteps. This regular pulse is enriched by off-the-beat rhythms in the bongos and guitar strum and the varied rhythmic accents of the singer and horns. While the "on-beatness" is unequivocal, the music is also rich and complex because of the interaction of different parts.

Rhythmic feel is the product, then, of interaction between different parts, not fully expressed in what is played by the bass, the guitar, the singer, or any one part. Calypso, like many dance musics of the African diaspora, is *polyrhythmic*, meaning that it features a constant rhythmic feel, or "groove," that is created by the interaction of repeating and contrasting parts. Diagram (a) in Activity 3.6 depicts the rhythmic interaction between different instrumental parts in David Rudder's "High Mas'" (see Activity 3.6). These rhythms are fairly typical of calypso generally, and you should spend the time to understand them well (see Activity 3.7). The interaction between the on-beat kick drum and the syncopated (i.e., "between-the-beat") keyboard strum produces the composite rhythm notated in Figure (b) in Activity 3.6. This bouncy exciting rhythm, produced by contrasting parts, is fundamental to all calypso music. The off-beat high hat is also standard in most calypso, and the pitter patter of the bells contributes to a dense texture that is typical of carnival street music. The patterns in Diagram (a) in Activity 3.6 are repeated throughout the song and can be referred to as "fixed rhythms."

ACTIVITY 3.6: CALYPSO RHYTHMIC FEEL IN "HIGH MAS'" *Diagram (a) depicts the rhythms of different instruments in your recording of "High Mas'" (CD track 9). All of these are "fixed rhythms," which means that they repeat throughout the song. Because they also contrast with each other they cre-*

ate an effect called polyrhythm—*a consistent background of re-peating, interlocking rhythms. The size and shading of the boxes in Diagram (a) indicate the relative "weight" the different in-struments have in our perception of the rhythm. You can read these rhythms in relation to the two "main beats" of the kick drum, counting the "in-between" beats as well:*

One-ee-and-ah **Two**-ee-and-ah

The strum then sounds, for example, on "ee," "ah," and "and":

One-**ee**-and-**ah** Two-ee-**and**-ah

The high hat falls on "and":

One-ee-**and**-ah Two-ee-**and**-ah

    *Note that the strum notated here is the second half of the key-board part on the recording of "High Mas'." The other half is like the high hat, so the full strum as you hear it on the record-ing is "One-ee-**and**-ah Two-ee-**and**-ah, One-**ee**-and-**ah** Two-ee-**and**-ah."*

(a)

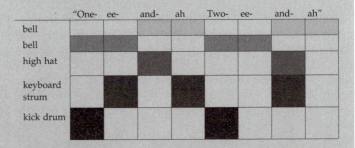

    The musical notation in Figure (b) represents a rhythm that you may hear emerging as a composite of the polyrhythmic com-bination in Diagram (a).

(b)

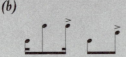

ACTIVITY 3.7: PERFORMING THE RHYTHMIC
FEEL   *Try to keep the steady pulse of the kick drum in your foot,
or better yet "chip" with both your feet, alternating while you clap
the strum. Using your mouth, can you also make the sizzling sound
of a cymbal ("tss . . . tss") on the high hat rhythm?*

PHRASING

The calypsonian's singing also contributes to the rhythmic feel, his variable rhythms constantly interacting with the fixed rhythm of the bass,
drums, guitar, and other instruments. One of the most important skills of
a calypso singer is his ability to phrase his lyrics in a way that gives punch
and flavor to the music. The Mighty Sparrow's vocal line in "Jean and Dinah," for example, is full of subtle pushing and pulling of time, as well as
crackling rhythmic phrases that drive the song forward (as when he in-
serts "So when you bounce up" to introduce the chorus). Try to match
Sparrow's phrasing when you sing the song yourself (see Activity 3.8).

ACTIVITY 3.8: "JEAN AND DINAH" PHRASING   *Many
musicians and musicologists use the word "phrasing" to refer to
the way a singer or an instrument creates segments in a melody
(where a singer takes breaths, for example) and gives them shape.
In Trinidad, however, "phrasing" refers specifically to the way a
singer or instrumentalist renders the rhythm of the melody.*

*Sing the chorus to "Jean and Dinah" (CD track 6) with care-
ful attention to rhythmic phrasing while you step to a steady beat.
Be sure, for example, to master the syncopation at the words "bet
you life is something they selling." When you have learned the
phrasing that way, try adding the strum rhythm in Figure (a) in
Activity 3.6 with hand claps. When you can do all this at once
you will have developed a holistic understanding of the rhythmic
feel in this song.*

BREAKS

Another variable event in many of these songs occurs at moments when the instruments come to a dramatic and unexpected stop, perhaps punch a rhythm together, and then resume the flow of their fixed rhythms. This is referred to as a "break," and it is an important device for creating excitement and rhythmic energy. A break is a momentary suspension of a kinetic energy that inexorably returns, and its excitement is most strongly felt in our bodies as an experience of movement and anticipation (see Activity 3.9). As such it is a common device in dance-oriented calypsoes and soca music.

ACTIVITY 3.9: BREAKS *In Super Blue's "Pump It Up" (CD track 1), an extended break on the repeated words "I wish I could" sets up the dancers to boost their energy to a new level when the fixed rhythm returns ith the words, "wine on you!"*

In the chorus of "High Mas'" (CD track 9), the music stops and Rudder sings by himself, "and if you know what I mean then scream!" Coming after several repeats of the phrase "if you know what I mean," this break makes a climactic and dramatic transition into the next section.

In the chorus of "Jean and Dinah" (CD track 6), the voices and all the fixed rhythmic parts stop at the words "don't make no ROW." A unison horn line fills the space, and then the voices and fixed rhythm resume.

≃

Calypso has become associated not just with carnival celebrations, where it is heard most often, but also with Trinidadian cultural identity generally. Many Trinidadians will tell you that it is their national music because it has a long association with carnival and communal festivity and because its lyrics contain an accumulated wealth of social and historical commentary. While calypso is the *genre* of music most often associated with Trinidad, however, the national *instrument* of Trinidad and Tobago is the steel pan, the subject of the next chapter.

CHAPTER 4

The National Instrument

∞

In 1992 Prime Minister Patrick Manning declared the steel pan Trinidad and Tobago's national instrument, giving official recognition to a sentiment that many Trinidadians had shared for a long time. "Pan," as most Trinidadians call the instrument, first became an emblem of intense pride for people in poor neighborhoods of Port of Spain and elsewhere, as the creative achievements of early panmen defied establishment efforts to suppress the steelbands. In the 1950s and 1960s, people of more diverse backgrounds came to identify with the accomplishments of steelband tuners and musicians, so that pan is today seen as something more than a signifier of lower-class communities and histories. According to mas' man (masquerade designer) Francisco Cabral, "Pan, calypso, and carnival are the only things we have to make us proud today and in the future; and of these, the only one we can claim entirely is pan. This is the cornerstone of our culture."[*]

It is common, of course, for musical genres, instruments, sounds, or lyrics to trigger feelings of belonging—of community, ethnic, or national identity—but in the case of the steelband this identity symbolism is particularly important. For Trinidadians who view the steel pan as a symbol of their nation and society, the telling of its history is a way of telling something about themselves. Different tellings give importance to different people, different neighborhoods, and different events. I begin this chapter with one person's account of the steel pan's origins and then go on to discuss the transformation of the steelband's social status—a story of struggle and triumph that makes pan a compelling symbol for the nation. Finally I discuss, in turn, the instrument, the ensemble, and steelband musical style.

Ganase, Pat (1993). "Return of the Savage." *Trinidad Guardian Magazine*. Port of Spain. April 25, p. 3

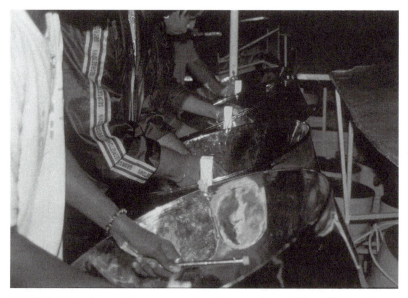

FIGURE 4.1 *A row of tenor pans played by members of Phase II Pan Groove. They are elevated on the float at the center of the band; other pans can be seen on the ground-level racks below them.*

ORIGINS

Many different stories exist concerning the invention of pan. Disagreements often occur between people from different neighborhoods or bands who want their stories to be acknowledged and remembered. It is almost impossible to determine a single "true" story of pan's invention, but listening to and reading different accounts gives one a vivid sense of the importance that many Trinidadians attach to this instrument. I will share one of these accounts, an interview that I did in March 1993 with the late Carleton "Zigilee" Constantine. As a teenager, Zigilee participated in the transition from *tamboo bamboo* to steelband and played with a band called Bar 20 from the Belmont neighborhood of Port of Spain. Later he played with City Syncopators and Casablanca. The basic elements of Zigilee's story are repeated in other people's accounts: steelbands evolved out of *tamboo bamboo* roughly around 1940; the innovators were young men from poor neighborhoods; competition was intense, expressing itself both in music and in violent "clashes" between bands; the early tuners had no formal music training; and neither police harassment nor public disapproval could extinguish the pan-men's passion for their new instrument.

Now the boom of the bamboo [the largest and deepest-pitched bam-boo tube, struck on the ground in a steady rhythm] it have tone but not plenty carry [volume]. That's why you find in the band you have five to six boomers. Then come the biscuit drum [a metal container used to ship biscuits]. The biscuit drum when it come in that's the first who invade the bamboo. When you hear that—more tone, eas-ier to carry. So it went on a little while, just about for a few weeks. So out go the boom. All the rest [of the bamboo instruments] hold on there for a little while, til a guy come with two piece of stick and he start to rattle on the side of the biscuit drum there. . . . So after a few days the cutter [the highest-pitched, improvising part] on this biscuit drum it have more volume than the old cutter, so out he went too.

So eventually now, the bamboo—problem. Cause we was young, and it had some older guys who like the bamboo. So what we used to do, they would be doing their thing in the yard, and we would come right there with the steelband and we would blow them off. Be-cause more volume. And when we start to pile the pressure on they start to sit down and quit, and all kind of names they call we. But eventually they give in to the long run, and all them they leave the bamboo, and steelband pick up from there.

It start off with like, this guy have a pan with two notes, you make one with three, and then a next one come with four and make your one into rubbish, and then one come with five, and you know we keep on. Till it had a certain time when the pan reach up to about nine notes. We never even had a scale. . . . We never know what we was looking for you know. We was looking for plenty notes because the main idea was like, you have one with four, and I looking for one with five, to make your own look like rubbish, you know. And they had a next guy waiting with six, you know. And that definitely was the competition at that time. I can remember when I make it seven, I go and hide my pan beneath the old lady bed. Well at least I was lucky because it make about two days before it was rubbish, and then a guy come out with more. It had seven notes, so being it had seven notes, you didn't want to let anyone else see it, you just want to be the boss. Well, it make at least two days. And then it come out be-cause it was rubbish.

Now when we was looking for notes, we just looking for notes, different tones. We don't know what we looking for, just something different when you hit the pan, and you bus' on that [i.e., repeat something that sounds good]. You don't know what the note was, but you just had seven. . . . When scale came in I could remember the time. But this was way back, now, because I was in Casablanca. When I was in Casablanca I had a pan, scales come, but what he coulda play on his own, I just couldn't play on mine. When I get to find the note he had, it was a G♯, and we used to call these notes "in-between." Til a man was even trying between E and F, and B and C. Man was still trying to get something because he just feel it have something between everything!

It reach nine notes in about a year and a half. I got lock up [arrested] in the year 1940. We just leave bamboo and we just gone into pan. That is the year when I got lock up. So all these things start to happen afterwards. 1941 or 1942.

Well the police was against pan. And anybody they see with a pan, they going to beat yuh and lock yuh up. . . . We had to battle with them because, you know, I definitely was from a poor family. We had nothing. And the onliest thing we get was this little thing to play. And the police was against that. Boy and they woulda had to kill we because it was all we had. . . . It was peaceful and quiet. As much as the pressure was, nobody used to thief and thing. But when these police come in and start to pile the pressure on, they turn everybody beast. Because we find that we shouldn't get locked for that at all. Just pan.

Although Zigilee's account indicates that pan—a metal container whose surface is tuned to several distinct pitches—was invented as early as 1940, pan was not often heard in public at first because of a ban on carnival during World War II. The new instrument was, in a sense, publicly consecrated at the 1946 carnival when Winston "Spree" Simon performed before the English governor, playing "Ave Maria," "God Save the King," and a number of local calypsoes on his metal *ping pong* (an onomatopoetic name for the early melody pans). In a colonial society that did not recognize drumming or call-and-response singing as music, the ability to play such recognizable melodies (to play, that is, the repertoires of other performers) conferred upon Simon and other panmen a status that previously they had been denied: that of musician.

CHANGING PERCEPTIONS

While pioneers of pan such as Spree Simon are honored today in stories, calypsoes, and official functions, they were not so popular when they first began to play these new metal instruments. Early steelbands did not have the resonant timbre or melodic versatility that we associate with the modern pan; their sound was still intensely percussive, and they included a large proportion of nonpitched instruments like motor vehicle brake drums, or "irons." Listen to the timbre of the pans, the playing of the irons, and the noise of the crowd in the steelband version of "Jean and Dinah" (CD track 7). This recording, made in the streets at 1956 carnival, conveys an idea of the festive and percussive sound of early steelband on the road.

Steelbands in the 1940s, which were more percussive still and less versatile melodically, were not necessarily appreciated for their artistic innovations. Indeed, for some people they were simply louder than the bamboo bands and therefore more bothersome, as suggested by this letter to a newspaper editor in 1946:

> [W]e must put up with the transformation of earth into bedlam, to the utter disgust of parents, students, tired workmen, troubled people and invalids. Can beating is pan beating in any language and in any form. It does nobody any good, and when it is indulged in all day all night, day in and day out, it is abominable. Why is there no legislation to control it? If it must continue and if by virtue of its alleged inherent beauty and charm it will someday bring popularity and fame to the island and a fortune to the beaters, then by all means let it go on—but in the forests and other desolate places. (C. W. Clarke, *Trinidad Guardian*, June 6, 1946)

This characterization of steelband music as abominable "can beating" reflects a Eurocentric aesthetic that did not recognize such percussive sounds as "music." Fear of bedlam in carnival was an obsession particularly of the English, as noted in Chapter 1. However, we don't know where C. W. Clarke might have fit into the hierarchy of class and race in 1940s Trinidad. He might have been a member of the white upper class. He might have been a "colored" man of mixed race with a good education and middle-class social status. He might even have been a black man living in one of the same neighborhoods as the panmen, a "tired workman" annoyed by the noise or perhaps upset at how the panmen's behavior reflected on his community. (Judging by its name, he probably was not of East Indian descent.) C. W. Clarke's opinions of the steelband reflected the views of the dominant authorities, but they might have been voiced by any person who resented the noise or the threat of violence that steelbands posed in his own neighborhood. In short, there was a general consensus in 1940s Trinidad that a "respectable" person would not have anything to do with a steelband.

On the other hand, Clarke's letter refers to the steelband's "alleged inherent beauty and charm." Who would have been alleging this in 1946? The collection and promotion of folk music and dance were important components of the nationalist movement, and already in the 1940s some intellectuals in Trinidad were holding up the steelband as an example of "urban folk" creativity. Some liberal politicians also saw steelband music as a constructive outlet for the energies of young men who, because of disadvantaged social circumstances, tended to engage in crime and violence. Both of these interests—the cultural and the sociological—prompted the 1949 formation of a Government Steelband Committee that helped establish the Trinidad and Tobago Steelband Association (today called Pan Trinbago) as well as a national steelband called the Trinidad All Steel Percussion Orchestra (TASPO), with representatives from different bands.

When TASPO traveled to London in 1951 to play at the Festival of Britain, the astonished praise heaped upon them by English newspapers enhanced the steelband's reputation back home in Trinidad. Following TASPO's success abroad, the steelband's cultural status continued to rise through increased middle-class involvement and government and commercial patronage. In the early 1950s middle-class boys from some of Port of Spain's elite secondary schools began to form their own bands, which some people referred to as "college boy" bands ("college" being the term for secondary schools in the British system). Bands such as Silver Stars and Dixieland gave boys from respectable families a chance to play pan, and before long their parents and neighbors were "jumping up" behind these steelbands at carnival, something that would have been considered both scandalous and dangerous for middle-class Trinidadians just a few years earlier. Women also got a start in this very male-dominated art form in the 1950s through the Girl Pat Steel Orchestra and a few other all-female bands, although it was not until the 1980s that women were integrated into the established bands to a significant extent. During the 1970s schools all over Trinidad began to include steelband in the curriculum, one of the most important ways in which the steelband has become legitimized as a cornerstone of Trinidad's national culture.

THE INSTRUMENT

At the center of all this excitement and change is a musical instrument that has a curious power to inspire and delight people. Trinidadians like to say that "pan is a jumbie," a supernatural spirit that possesses people. How are we to explain this irresistible appeal? What made pan so different from anything that had been heard before? The most exciting innovation at the beginning, as Zigilee recounts, was the tuning of distinct pitches on a single metal surface. In the long run, however, an even more astonishing achievement was the sound, or timbre, of the instrument.

The percussive sound of the early pans was, by the late 1960s, replaced by a bell-like tone that inspired comparisons to an organ or even a choir of human voices. You can hear the difference in timbre yourself between the 1956 steelband version of "Jean and Dinah" (CD track 7) and the 1986 recording of Phase II Pan Groove's "Backline" (CD track 13). Technically speaking, the timbre of the modern steel pan differs from early pans in two important respects. First, the notes are tuned carefully to include *harmonics*—high notes that sound simultaneously with the fundamental pitch and make the note sound brighter (see Activity 4.1). The other important difference between early pans and modern pans is the *sustain*—the length of time that a note continues to sound after it is struck. On early pans, players could hold one pitch for an extended duration by "rolling" it (striking repeatedly with both sticks in rapid alternation), but the sound of the individual mallet strokes created a distinctly percussive effect. On a modern pan, the lingering resonance of a single stroke and the seamless sustain of rolled notes, especially in the lower registers, more closely approximate the flowing quality of the human voice or an instrument such as the violin or saxophone.

ACTIVITY 4.1: STEEL PAN HARMONICS *If you have access to a pan, try hearing the harmonics on one of its larger notes. You will find that the fundamental pitch sounds most strongly when you strike in the center; if you strike gently around the edges of the note, perhaps with a wooden stick instead of a rubber one, you will hear very high pitches as well. These are the harmonics or overtones that help to give the note its distinctive bright timbre (sound quality).*

Before pan tuners could worry about matching the sustain and timbre of "conventional" instruments, however, they had to create pans that had all the same pitches that those instruments had. Early ping pongs, such as the ones described by Zigilee and played in 1946 by Spree Simon, were made by pounding out the surface of a paint can or some other metal container into a convex shape and raising several bumps on this surface. These bumps were tuned to different pitches that sounded when struck with a wooden stick. The first ping pongs had only two or three notes, and early pan tuners created brief but interesting melodies using the pitches they heard in the chimes of the clock tower at Queens Royal College or the bugles that were used in some early steelbands. One of the first songs played on a steel pan was "Mary Had a Little Lamb" because the song uses only four different pitches. Tuners soon added more notes to their ping pongs so that they could play other songs that had more pitches.

Pans like the "cuatro," the "grundig," and the "grumbler" were developed to accompany the ping pong melody in a lower register with repetitive rhythmic/harmonic patterns. Early versions of these pans were made from a Bermudez biscuit drum, about two feet high and two feet across. The "boom," named after its bamboo predecessor, was the lowest-pitched instrument. Early booms called "cuff booms" functioned much like bass drums, but they soon were tuned to play bass lines of just two, three, or four notes. The caustic soda drum, which had a deep sound and yet was light enough to carry and play while walking, soon became a favorite container for this "tune boom," or bass, as it was later called. These various accompanying instruments came to be referred to as "background" pans to distinguish them from melody-carrying "frontline" pans such as the ping pong. Unlike the earliest ping pongs, the surfaces of later pans were sunk into a concave bowl, and they were struck with rubber-tipped mallets to produce a more mellow sound. By around 1950, the fifty-five-gallon oil drum (available in abundance because of the presence of a local oil industry and a U.S. naval base) became the standard material for most pans.

In the 1950s all pans became chromatic, meaning that they had all the "in-between" notes that Zigilee talked about (i.e., the sharps and flats, or the notes that correspond to the black keys on a piano). This meant more notes on every pan; since lower notes need more space, chromatic background pans had to be tuned in sets of multiple drums. First came the triple bass, then the double seconds (Figure 4.2), then triple cellos (Figure 4.3), with many variations following over the years (Figure 4.4). Initially these multiple pans could be used only on stage; on the road steelband musicians played single pans that were suspended by a strap around their necks as they walked. In the late 1950s, however, North Stars' tuner Anthony Williams built racks on wheels so

FIGURE 4.2   *Tuner Lloyd Gay puts the finishing touches on a chromed set of double seconds outside his workshop in Gasparillo.*

that musicians could play a set of multiple pans while supporters pushed the instruments along the road.

The modern steelband features a wide variety of instruments with different ranges and different patterns of note placement (e.g. Figures 4.3 and 4.4). Many bands still use pans with unique patterns that their own tuners have invented. However, certain patterns have gained popularity in almost all the bands, so there is an increasing degree of standardization in tuning. The circle of fifths tenor and the double seconds, tuned in complementary whole tone scales (Figure 4.5) are two of the most common patterns.

FIGURE 4.3   *A set of cellos tuned in three complementary diminished chords. No-tice that the skirt is cut longer than that of the tenors and seconds to help the reso-nance of the lower-pitched notes.*

FIGURE 4.4   *Barry Nanton of Desperadoes steelband plays a set of nine-bass.*

ACTIVITY 4.2: PATTERNS OF TENOR AND DOUBLE SECOND PANS (FROM THOMAS 1990)

There are several styles of tenor pan, differing in their range and note placement, but one of the most common designs the "circle of fifths" (top). This is a term from formal music theory, referring to the interval of a fifth—the distance between that are five steps apart in the scale. If you keep progressing through a series of notes that are a 5th apart you will end up with the note you started on: for example, C-G-D-A-E-B-F♯-C♯-G♯-E♭-B♭-F-C. On the tenor pan these notes are placed around the rim of the drum, giving a new meaning to the term "circle" of 5ths.

The double seconds (bottom) is a set of two separate pans, dividing all the notes of the scale into two "whole tone" scales—scales in which each successive note is the same distance, or interval from the last. Two complementary whole tone scales provide all the notes of the chromatic scale, and the chromatic scale can be played very easily on the double seconds, since the left and right hands alternate throughout: C-C♯-D-E♭-E-F-F♯-G-G♯-G-B♭-B-C.

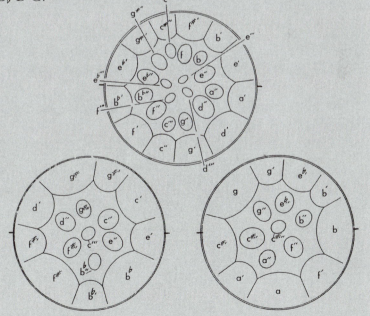

FIGURE 4.5 *Patterns of tenor and double second pans.*

Steelpan builders, known as "tuners," are the heroes of pan's invention, and many of the legendary steelband leaders in the early years of pan were tuners: Spree Simon of Destination Tokyo steelband, Neville Jules of Trinidad All Stars, Ellie Mannette of Invaders, Anthony Williams of North Stars, and Rudolph Charles of Desperadoes.

THE ENSEMBLE

A number of established instrumental ensembles can be cited as models for the steelband. The basic three-part texture of the steelband (discussed at more length later) parallels the textural organization of a *tamboo bamboo* ensemble: a high-pitched instrument plays a variable leading part and midrange instruments play contrasting fixed rhythms, supported by a sparse repetitive "boom" below. Specific rhythms from *tamboo bamboo* also have been transferred onto metal instruments and other steelband percussion such as the congas and drumset. The influence of Venezuelan string bands is evident in the early borrowing of the instrument name "cuatro" and in the use of the term "strumming" to describe the rhythmic/harmonic patterns played by background pans. Another important model was the instrumentation and terminology of European classical music, which explains why the "ping pong" became the "tenor," "grumbler" and "grundig" became "guitar" or "cello," and "boom" became "bass."

Although a few small steelbands (five or six players) perform at hotels and other entertainment venues, most community-based steelbands in Trinidad field around a hundred players at carnival time. They usually also have smaller "stage sides" of ten to thirty players that play for fetes or other events in the off-season. Whatever its specific choice of pans, the band is arranged in sections of similar instruments—tenors, seconds, guitars, basses, and so on—with the tenor section always largest, so as to project the melody strongly.

Nonpitched percussion instruments in a steelband are collectively referred to as the "engine room." The term probably comes from the engine room of ocean-going ships and is an apt metaphor for the driving force provided by the percussion at the heart of a steelband. While preferences vary from band to band, the most common instruments in the engine room are drumset, congas (played with rubber-tipped mallets), several large metal scrapers, and a number of ear-piercing irons struck with metal bolts or rods. Irons (Figure 1.4) were originally brake drums from cars and trucks, but they are often custom-made for steelbands today. At the Panorama competition, the engine room is placed at the

FIGURE 4.6 *The float for Renegades steelband is steered through the crowd toward the Panorama stage. Congas and drumset are placed at the center, tenor pans along the edge, and irons at ground level. The miniature oil tower at the front signifies Renegades' sponsor, Amoco oil company.*

very center of the band on an elevated trailer, or "float," that pulsates visibly with the rhythm of the percussionists. Indeed, the steelband has to be seen as well as heard to be fully appreciated—its chromed instruments, the architecture of its canopied pan racks, and animated pan beaters all contribute to an exciting visual spectacle (Figure 4.6).

THE MUSIC

Steelband musical style is related in important ways to calypso—indeed, both steelband and calypso music respond to the same Trinidadian traditions of dance and carnival festivity. Your steelband recording of "Jean and Dinah" (CD track 7), for example, shares many of the features of the calypso road march, as discussed in Chapter 3. Note, for example, the constant patter of the irons, similar to the the bells in the diagram in Activity 3.6. This band chose to arrange only the chorus of the Mighty Sparrow's song because that is the most catchy and well-known part of the melody. The people following the band sometimes join in singing (you can hear this faintly at the end of the recorded excerpt), and the chorus is also fun for dancers because of the break.

Despite the close stylistic relationship between steelband music and calypso, however, the steelband has developed many conventions of its own. The bass line in the steelband version of "Jean and Dinah" is one example. It plays a pattern that evolved on the simple three- or four-note booms of the early steelband, similar to the calypso bass line in its on-beat feel, but not "walking" as smoothly (Figure 4.7).

Strumming patterns, chord voicings, melodic phrasing, and other steelband musical practices have also developed in ways that are uniquely suited to the instrument. Many of the rhythmic conventions of the steelband are derived from neo-African percussion ensembles such as Shango drumming and *tamboo bamboo*. The polyrhythmic concept that characterizes these ensembles (repetitive interlocking parts that create a constant rhythmic texture, supporting vocal or instrumental improvisation) is still fundamental to the steelband, particularly in the playing of the "irons."

A group of iron men (anywhere from three to six in a large band) playing interlocking patterns comprise the most important part of the steelband engine room. The piercing sound of the irons is a reference that helps to coordinate all the players in the band rhythmically. In the early days of the steelband, the irons were especially important for the volume and power they provided during musical clashes with other bands in the streets. In CD track 7, you can hear how the irons drive the rhythm and dominate the sound of the band.

Iron players typically play two or three contrasting parts, a practice they refer to as "plaiting" or "braiding the rhythm" (Activity 4.3)—what musicologists would call polyrhythm. One of the players is usually designated as the "cutter," improvising on top of the other fixed patterns to create changes in volume, excitement, or tension. The iron players usually play the same fixed patterns in every piece, changing only to coordinate with the pans at breaks, to fill a space, or to add occasional excitement or energy. If you listen carefully to the iron in CD track 7 you will hear these breaks, fills, and slight variations in an otherwise constant accompaniment.

FIGURE 4.7 *Early bass line.*

ACTIVITY 4.3: BRAIDING THE IRONS *The notated parts in the accompanying figure demonstrate one common way of braiding three irons and are another example of polyrhythm. The first two parts are fixed rhythms. The third part, a constant "off-beat" pulse, is what the cutter usually plays, varying his part at important moments in the arrangement. You can reproduce these rhythms nicely on bottles tuned to different pitches with water and struck with a spoon ("bottle and spoon" was a favorite instrument in the* tamboo bamboo *bands). Play the first part on the lowest-pitched bottle, the second part on a middle pitch, and the cutter on the highest pitch. As you play, tap your foot or chip together as a common point of reference, and concentrate on keeping your own part steady while listening to how it fits with the others. Because of the different pitches, the composite is an exciting sort of melody, as well as a rhythm.*

First iron

Second iron

Cutter

In contrast to the consistent patterns of the irons, the pan players play much more varied parts, which are composed and coordinated by an arranger. Phase II Pan Groove's recording of "Back Line" (CD track 13) provides a good example of typical steelband arranging techniques, which I describe under the broad headings of form, texture, and rhythm.

Form. Steelband pieces are often arrangements of songs, and so they tend to follow the strophic, or verse-and-chorus, form typical of calypso and so much other popular song. Without the lyrics, of course, instrumental arrangements tend to be more repetitive than the vocal versions. For staged competition performances arrangers create elaborate varia-

FIGURE 4.8 *Len "Boogsie" Sharpe supervising a rehearsal of Phase II Pan Groove.*

tions to avoid this repetition, as we shall see in Chapter 5. For dancing and parties, on the other hand, repetition can be a virtue, and steelband arrangers may simply repeat the same melody over a few times. "Back Line" is an original composition for steelband by arranger Len "Boogsie" Sharpe (Figure 4.8); even though it was never performed with lyrics, it has a verse and chorus form, which we can describe as AB— or, more accurately, as AABB because each section is repeated. In CD track 13 you can hear the Introduction (also repeated), AA, BB, and then A begins to repeat at the end as it fades out (see Activity 4.4).

ACTIVITY 4.4: TEXTURE IN "BACK LINE" *Try to distinguish these different layers of texture in Phase II's recording of "Back Line" (CD track 13): (1) the high-pitched tenors playing melody, (2) the lowest-pitched basses playing a steady bass line, and (3) midrange pans strumming.*

Next listen to the "A" section alone at a slower tempo (CD track 14), performed by my students and friends at the University of Washington. This is a much smaller group (six people instead of twenty-five), with only a pair of conga drums instead of the whole engine room. Each time the "A" section is repeated, a new part is added, so you can better distinguish the individual parts (which I transcribed as closely as possible from Phase II's recording):

1. Bass pans playing bass line.
2. Base + double second pans strumming chords. (Notice that the seconds' strum is constantly off-beat, contrasting with the on-beat pulse of the bass.)
3. Bass + double seconds + tenor pan playing melody.
4. Bass + double second + tenor + double tenor doubling melody at octave. The double tenor is a pan very similar to the seconds; notice how it adds depth and power to the melody by playing it in a lower register.
5. Base + double seconds + tenor + double tenor + triple cellos strumming chords (played twice). Cellos enrich the harmony and play a strum that contrasts somewhat with the seconds; you can hear the low-pitched cello strum best in the second half the "A" section.

How well could you distinguish the parts before you were able to listen to them separately? Listen again to Phase II's recording and see if you hear the different layers of texture more clearly. Although melody is often the easiest part to identify, the rest of the texture provides the harmony, rhythm, and timbre that greatly influence how one hears and feels music.

Texture. Texture refers to the relationship between parts. The conventional terminology of "frontline" (referring to the tenor pans, as well as double tenors and seconds when they are playing melody) and "background" (referring to the lower-pitched strumming pans and the basses) suggests a two-layered conception of steelband orchestration. However, the strumming pans and bass are quite different in character, so it is more useful to think of a simple steelband arrangement as having *three* distinct layers: melody, strummed chords, and bass line (refer again to Activity 4.3).

Rhythm. The strumming of the midrange pans creates a textural contrast in the overall ensemble, and the choice of individual strumming patterns also affects the rhythmic character of the music. In general, strums tend to avoid the "main beats" (as you saw with the calypso keyboard strum in the diagram in Activity 3.6), creating a syncopated contrast to the more on-beat bass line. Often two different sections of the band will strum with different notes and different rhythms, a practice that parallels the polyrhythmic braiding of the irons. In the recording of the individual parts in "Back Line" (CD track 14) you can hear how the cellos' and seconds' strumming patterns contrast with each other. There are also moments when the strumming changes, giving a different rhythmic feel to different parts of the piece. During the first phrase of the "A" section, for example, there is a sharp strumming accent on the up-beat (just after the main beat), and then the strumming becomes smoother in the last phrase.

A significant change in the rhythmic feel is produced at the beginning of the "B" section, where the bass and kick drum switch from an on-beat "walking" pulse to an off-beat pattern. This sets up a sort of tension that resolves deliciously when a smooth walking bass returns in the second phrase of "B." The off-beat bass pattern at the beginning of "B" is associated with soca music (Chapter 6), so this arrangement might be described as alternating between a calypso feel and a soca feel (see Activity 4.5).

ACTIVITY 4.5: SOCA FEEL IN "BACK LINE" (CD TRACK 13) *Listen to how the bass changes its rhythm at the beginning of the "B" section. You can perform this rhythm by tapping four beats with your foot and doing a double clap on beats 2 and 4: (1), 2-and, (3), 4-and. This rhythm is often played in soca music by the bass and/or the kick drum.*

Do you hear where the bass returns to a more even on-beat pattern? How would you describe how that change in rhythmic feel makes you feel, emotionally and physically?

∞

The proclamation of pan as Trinidad's "national instrument" honors the achievements of pan tuners and musicians and celebrates the distinctive instruments and music of the steelband. At the same time, pan links Trinidad and Tobago with the music and instruments of other nations. It is common to hear the steel pan described, for example, as "the only musical instrument invented in the twentieth century," a phrase that claims a special place for pan in a global order of musical instruments. As the story of TASPO demonstrates, pride in local ingenuity goes hand in hand with pride in the ability of Trinidadian musicians to make a good impression in an international musical culture. One of the most dramatic expressions of this pride is the broad variety of musical genres that steelband musicians have learned to play. This repertoire, and the way it varies to suit different venues, is the subject of the next chapter.

CHAPTER 5

Steelband Repertoire

∞

In an important sense, the origin of the steelband as something new is marked by the ability of early pioneers like Zigilee and Spree Simon to cross over into new repertoires, from the carnival *lavways* of the *tamboo bamboo* ensemble to songs and instrumental pieces that were associated with other ensembles. It was the ambition to play a Lord Kitchener calypso, a Perez Prado mambo, or a Beethoven minuet that motivated tuners to develop an instrument of such versatility. As the instruments developed chromatic tuning, the possibilities of repertoire became ever greater. By 1951, TASPO's concert repertoire included Johannes Brahms' "Cradle Song," the "Tennessee Waltz," Perez Prado's "Mambo Jambo," and many other diverse compositions. This kind of variety was characteristic of staged concerts (such as TASPO's performance at the Festival of Britain) played in halls and auditoriums, where steelbands showcased the breadth of their repertoire. A variety of other venues also played an important role in the development of steelband music, and each of these venues had distinctive conventions of style and repertoire.

MUSIC FOR THE ROAD

When steelbands took over from *bamboo tamboo* they inherited the function of providing musical accompaniment to dance and masquerade. Many of the steelbands in Trinidad were originally associated with neighborhood masquerade bands, and they competed with the brass bands of the more affluent masqueraders for control of the streets at carnival. (The term "brass band" is used in Trinidad for carnival bands that may feature not only a brass section, but also guitar, bass, keyboard, and drums.) Military masquerade themes, especially sailor mas' (Figure 1.2), were especially popular with the steelbands, but some of them also were associated with more elaborate masquerades based on historical, literary, or cultural themes. Silver Stars won Band of the Year (i.e., masquerade band) in 1963 with the theme of Gulliver's Travels, the only steelband ever to achieve this honor.

In carnival performances, diverse genres of music are rendered by steelbands in the fairly uniform style described in Chapter 4—a style that responds to the particular kind of dancing and festivity associated with carnival masquerade. Hence we must define the kind of music steelbands play on the road in terms of style, rather than genre. Calypso has always been an important part of the steelbands' repertoire for the road, but it is not the only genre that steelbands draw on at carnival time. Steelbands also play pop songs from the United States and other countries, film music, and Latin American music. The mambos of Pérez Prado were especially popular with steelbands in the 1950s, and even classical music has been played at carnival (see the discussion of "the bomb" later in this chapter). During carnival, all of these genres were played with a road march rhythm and texture.

The variety of music steelbands played on the road had a significant influence on calypso musical style. By the late 1950s, steelbands were the most popular kind of music for carnival masquerade (having surpassed the brass bands), and the Road March title was given to the tune that the steelbands most enjoyed playing on carnival day. Since calypsonians needed the steelbands to popularize their songs, they began to compose with steelband arranging in mind. Calypsoes written for the steelband included more harmonic and melodic variety, as well as exciting melodic hooks that would sound good on pan.

One of Lord Kitchener's melodic hooks in "Pan in A Minor" (CD track 12) is the answer to the chorus of "beat pan," which he varies a bit each time with the changing words. This melody is played in a more fixed version on a steel pan in the instrumental section at the beginning of your example.

Beat pan
Boogsie on the tenor;
Beat pan
Bringing out the minor
Beat pan
Up come the Professor;
Beat pan
To add to de fire
Beat pan
I calling on Bradley;

Beat pan
To challenge Beverly
Beat pan
Which mean Desperado;
Beat pan
Go answer Tokyo

Another melodic phrase that is obviously intended for rendition on pan is the repeating melody of the rapid-fire words:

You gonna hear them at their best,
They will be going through a test,
You're gonna hear them as they pass

Songs such as this one, which were composed with the pan in mind, have become recognized as a particular type of calypso referred to as a "pan tune" (see Activity 5.1). In addition to their melodic and harmonic suitability for steelband arrangement, pan tunes are often characterized by lyrics that praise or comment upon the steelbands and their music. The very topic of Lord Kitchener's "Pan in A Minor" (CD track 12) is the singer's effort to write innovative music for the steelband:

They say to me they want a musical change in pan,
Well I didn't tell them yes,
But I didn't tell them no,
I say, well, gentlemen I gon' do the best I can,
As long as you challenge me
Well I going to have a go—
They all indicated that they were getting bored
And they would appreciate something new
So I thought it best to change to the minor chord,
To see really who is who

ACTIVITY 5.1: PAN TUNE FEATURES *Lord Kitchenere's "Pan in A Minor" (CD track 12) demonstrates several features, which you should be able to identify as you listen, that are common to many pan tunes.*

1. Its lyrics are about the steelband.

2. Its form consists of numerous sections that are harmonically distinctive so that they can be recognized in instrumental

variations. In this case you should be able to identify four distinct sections, which we will call A, B, C, and D.

3. It includes an exciting break. Here the break comes to introduce the C section, "Beat pan."

4. Its chorus (C) has a call-and-response form with a catchy melody, from which a steelband arranger can build an exciting jam.

Kitchener also calls the names of prominent arrangers (see the chorus quoted earlier)—Len "Boogsie" Sharpe, Ken "Professor" Philmore, Clive Bradley, and Beverly Griffith—and popular bands—Desperadoes and Destination Tokyo.

Steelbands playing arrangements of Kitchener's songs won more than half the Panorama competitions (nineteen out of thirty-seven) between 1963 and Kitchener's death in 2000, and "Pan in A Minor" is considered one of Kitchener's classic pan tunes (although oddly it did not win Panorama). Pan tunes in general are more likely today to be heard in Panorama (discussed later) than on the road. This is because steelbands have lost their place as the preferred music for masquerade; they have been replaced by recorded music played at intense volume on moving DJ trucks (Chapter 6).

FÊTES

Before DJ trucks and recorded music gained wide popularity in the late 1970s, steelbands were popular not only on the road but at pre-carnival fêtes as well. Fêtes—parties where people go to dance and socialize—are held by private individuals, commercial promoters, and various kinds of organizations throughout the period between New Year and carnival. Music for fêtes is similar to music for the road in that it is geared toward dancing. Fêtes today feature fast-paced soca music almost exclusively, played by amplified brass bands with singers. In the 1960s and 1970s, however, when the steelbands were at the height of their popularity, fêtes often included slow dances or Latin dances. A steelband's repertoire for fêtes therefore had to be more diverse than its repertoire for the road, which is still true today. Not all steelbands have the combination of diverse repertoire and danceable style that is required for fêtes. Even in the heyday of the steelband's popularity just a few steelbands got regular work at fêtes, but most steelbands still play in this context occasionally.

MUSIC FESTIVAL

In 1952 a steelband category was created at Trinidad's biennial Music Festival, a venue dedicated mainly to the performance of European art music. After 1980 this steelband competition continued as a separate steelband event called "Pan Is Beautiful" (Figure 5.1), and in 2000 it was renamed the "World Steelband Music Festival" and opened up to steelbands from other nations. In contrast to the steelbands' carnival repertoire, which is weighted toward dance genres like calypso and mambo, Music Festival performances give the steelbands a chance to perform a broader repertoire, especially European art music. The ambition to master the "Classics," as steelband musicians refer to this music, drove the development of the instrument. Pan tuners received advice from for-

FIGURE 5.1   *Trinidad All Stars steelband, one of the most accomplished performers of classical music for pan, plays at the 1992 Pan Is Beautiful music festival in Mucurapo Stadium.*

mally trained musicians on chromatic tuning patterns that could facilitate this repertoire and strove for a more and more resonant tone in their instruments. The Classics also challenged players to learn dynamics, articulation, and other skills that were little needed in calypso performances.

The steelband Music Festival today is held in a sports stadium in which five or six large steelbands can set up at the same time. The musicians dress in elegant matching attire, sometimes even formal jackets and ties; enter the stadium in single file; and stand at attention behind their instruments to await the conductor. In the manner of a European orchestra concert, the conductor stands on a podium and cues the musicians by waving his baton. A panel of judges listens to one band play its selections, awards points, and then moves to the next band. Adjudicators for the Music Festival always include one foreign music expert, which is thought to limit the problem of favoritism and also to assure international standards of musical excellence.

Each band plays three selections: a test piece, composed especially for the Music Festival and played by every band; a calypso, which is usually an arrangement from the Panorama competition of a previous year; and a tune of choice, which is almost always a piece by a European art music composer such as Beethoven, Mozart, Tchaikovsky, or Stravinsky. The Classics are usually symphonies written for a European orchestra, and an arranger must decide how to divide the parts for violins, cellos, flutes, french horns, and other instruments between the different instruments of the steelband. For this task, steelbands rely on help from formally trained musicians. This became one of the first roles available to women in the major steelbands, as far back as the 1960s. Women who have made important contributions as steelband arrangers for the festival include Merle Albino DeCoteau, Pat Bishop, and Dawn Batson.

The Music Festival provides an opportunity for steelbands to play a varied repertoire in a formal concert atmosphere. Some steelband enthusiasts prefer to hear steelband music in the festive atmosphere of carnival. Others, however, including most of the musicians, see the festival—particularly the performance of Classics—as an exciting and valuable musical challenge. Over the years the Festival has provided an important opportunity for steelband musicians to broaden their repertoire and skills. It is also seen as a chance for musicians to prove themselves by international standards of musicianship, a function underscored by the recent inclusion of steelbands from other countries.

THE BOMB

A competition known as the "Bomb," which was extremely popular in the 1950s and 1960s, provided a very different setting for the performance of European Classics. The Bomb grew out of musical rivalries in which steelbands attempted to outdo one another with performances of foreign songs set to calypso rhythm. Latin American music, especially the mambos of Pérez Prado, became popular for steelbands on the road in the early 1950s, with the rhythmic structure of the mambo adapted to the conventions of the steelband road march. Steelbands later adapted classical music in the same way, as well as movie songs and other foreign tunes. Bands began to rehearse these tunes secretly in order to surprise the crowds and upstage their rivals on *j'ouvert* Monday morning, the first day of carnival, a practice that became known as "dropping the Bomb." Beethoven's "Minuet in G," originally written for piano, was one of the first Bombs, performed by the Trinidad All Stars in the 1958 carnival (Figure 5.2).

Since Beethoven's minuet was in triple meter, the All Stars had to significantly transform the melody to make it fit the duple rhythm of a steelband road march. This sort of transformation of a piece raises interesting questions about the identity of a musical composition and how its meanings may change in different performance settings. A classical music composition like "Minuet in G" tends to be associated with formal stage performances and with European aesthetics and cultural values; but when a steelband performs it in a calypso style people relate to it very differently, dancing to the music instead of sitting and listening quietly.

For some nationalists in the 1960s, the cultural identity of the music was still determined more by the composer than by the style of performance. For example, a journalist named Pete Simon wrote, "Isn't this preference for the classics by steelbandsmen during this tempo-setting

FIGURE 5.2   *All Stars' "Minuet in G" versus Beethoven's version.*

period of our National Festival a clearcut attempt to downgrade the calypso? To relegate it to second choice? To give it an inferior place?"* Simon and others thought that the steelband, which was a unique symbol of Trinidadian culture, should play "Trinidadian" music at carnival.
But is calypso more Trinidadian than a Beethoven minuet arranged as
a road march? To put it another way, is genre (minuet) or composer
(Beethoven) a more important indicator of cultural identity than is style
(road march) or performer (Trinidad All Stars)? This question about
repertoire had very important consequences for steelband music because of the way it shaped the Panorama competition, which today is
the most important venue for steelband performance.

PANORAMA

In 1963, for the first carnival after Independence, the Carnival Development Commission, along with the steelband association, established
a new competition for steelbands called Panorama (Figure 5.3).
Panorama brought a new kind of restriction on repertoire, requiring
steelbands to play a calypso from the current year. This rule was seen
by many as a nationalist corrective to the "foreign" repertoire of the
Bomb competition. Panorama provided new sources of income from
prizes, appearance fees, and commercial sponsorship and also brought
the steelbands a new degree of exposure and prestige, showcasing them
on the same Queen's Park Savannah stage where the Carnival Queen
and Calypso Monarch competitions were held. By the 1980s Panorama
came to consume most of the steelbands' time and energy, a development that reflected the appeal of the competition as well as the increasing popularity of the DJs, who had begun to deprive steelbands of
work in other venues.

The Panorama competition is held in a series of stages stretched out
over a month (preliminaries, semifinals, zone finals), with the final
round on the Saturday night before carnival. The venue for most of
these events is the Queen's Park Savannah, a vast, roughly oval-shaped
area of open fields and trees, almost three miles in circumference, at the
base of the hills that border Port of Spain on the north. On the paved
track that approaches the stage, steelbands practicing their arrangements are surrounded by thick crowds of people who enjoy the chance
to mingle with the musicians. When its turn comes, each steelband hur-

---

Simon, P. (1970). *Trinidad Guardian*. Port of Spain. February 1, p. 5.

FIGURE 5.3 *Arranger Clive Bradley conducting the Desperadoes steelband at the 2000 Panorama semifinals.*

riedly rolls its mobile pan racks up a ramp and arranges them into a tight formation on the stage, while the vocal version of its calypso blares from loudspeakers. A traffic light at the end of the stage signals the recorded music to stop by changing from red to green, and the band is announced on the PA system. At the sound of a single stroke on an iron or cowbell, the whole band bows in unison; another stroke brings them back up. Now everyone has sticks in hand, some fidgeting nervously, others jumping, slapping hands and clapping their neighbors on the back, getting fired up as they wait for the starting count. Finally the players turn to their pans and their bodies rock with the rhythm, the crowd bracing for the sound of a steelband exploding, as a single iron sounds out the starting count. . . .

This elaborate ritual could not have been imagined at the time of the first Panorama competition, when the steelbands passed the judges on the move, performing in essentially the same way as they did on the road. Important musical innovations in that first Panorama, however, marked the beginning of a very different kind of steelband performance. North Stars's leader Tony Williams, in particular, borrowed several formal ideas from the symphony, including key changes (modulation) and theme and variation form. In European art music, "theme and varia- tion" form refers to a series of new or modified melodies composed over the same chord progression. A similar principle (although not usu- ally called by that name) is used by jazz musicians who play a com- posed melody and then improvise new melodies over the same chord progression. Following this general principle, North Stars played the verse and chorus of the Mighty Sparrow's "Dan Is the Man," then played two successive variations over the same chords.

In the wake of North Stars's success, other arrangers added other ideas to what some people call, for better or worse, a "formula" for Panorama arrangements. The dominant aspect of this formula contin- ues to be theme and variation form, because the audience expects to hear some reference to the original calypso throughout. Arrangers in- terrupt the strict sequence of variations, however, with new material for transitions, key changes, and "jams." Jams are sections in which a simple sequence of two to four chords is repeated over and over, often with a constant bass line or some other ostinato part, while a succes- sion of exciting rhythmic and melodic licks is played on top of this. We will focus on one specific example to illustrate the general pattern of a Panorama arrangement.

In the 1987 Panorama competition the Renegades played an arrange- ment of Lord Kitchener's song "Pan in A Minor," arranged by Jit Sama- roo (Figure 5.4). Samaroo, one of the most successful Panorama arrangers, is known for a very dense style, with fast runs in all the pans, even the basses, that show off the players' dexterity. Once you have be- come familiar with the vocal version (Activity 5.1; CD track 12), listen to the Renegades' version (Activity 5.2; CD track 15). Concentrate es- pecially on following the form, focusing on the relationship between the original verse and chorus and its subsequent variations.

ACTIVITY 5.2: FORM OF RENEGADES' "PAN IN A MINOR" *Jit Samaroo's arrangement of "Pan in A Minor" for Renegades steelband (CD track 15) is based on the idea of theme and variation. The theme here is the melody of Kitchener's original calypso. Variations are made by repeating the chord pro- gression of the theme but changing the melody. In Panorama arrangements like this one there are always various interruptions* *(introduction and coda, modulations, interludes, jams, etc.) in the repetition of the chord progression.*

0:00   Introduction, ending with rising chromatic run (key of a minor)

0:43   Verse and chorus (ABCDCD)

2:13   First variation $(A^1B^1A^1B^1C^1D^1C^1D^1)$

4:12   Modulation (to f minor)

4:16   Second variation $(A^2B^2A^2B^2C^2D^2C^2D^2)$

6:17   Interlude, with "James Bond" motive in background, modulation (to A♭ major)

6:30   Third variation $(A^3B^3C^3$ extended, D3, modulation to a♭ minor)

7:37   Interlude and modulation (back to a minor)

7:52   Fourth variation (A^4B^4)

8:22   Opening unison phrase from Kitchener recording

8:30   Fourth variation cont'd. (C^4, D^4)

9:00   Short jam based on C section, with percussion breaks

9:22   Opening unison phrase again

9:26   Coda, using motive from 'A'

Members of the audience at Panorama expect to be surprised and thrilled by the arranger's inventiveness, but they also expect to enjoy a song they already know, so arrangers must balance their elaborate effects and orchestrations with these kinds of constant references to the original vocal version. Samaroo takes a bit of license with the original form by repeating the AB section in the first two variations, by adding few extra bars in his transitions and modulations between variations, and by extending the C section into a jam in a couple of spots. Otherwise, the arrangement maintains a clear relationship to the original song by adhering to its chord progression and sectional structure.

Samaroo's variations also incorporate parts of Kitchener's melody to keep listeners reminded of the original song. He sometimes has the tenors play part of the melody at the beginning of a variation. He also likes to put the original tune into the background pans while the tenors play something different, as at the beginning of the second variation (minute 4:16 CD track 15). He also does this at the beginning of the

FIGURE 5.4 *Renegades' arranger Jit Samaroo.*

fourth variation (minute 7:52), when the background pans play just the answering melody that corresponds to the words "Well I didn't tell them yes, But I didn't tell them no." He may also quote a brief motive from the song at less predictable moments—at the song's very end, for example, the opening motive is repeated twice (minute 9:34). These references to Kitchener's melody, along with the chord progression and sectional structure of the original song, give the audience a strong sense that it is hearing a variation on something familiar.

One place where the thread of the original song may be obscured, however, is the jam, where the cyclical form and call and response draw the listener into a very different experience of time and musical form. The jams in this Jit Samaroo arrangement are short—they are mainly limited to variations on the call-and-response "C" section of Kitchener's original, plus a more dramatic sequence of breaks near the end (minute 9:00). Other Panorama arrangers like to dwell in cyclical jams for even more extended periods. Even in Samaroo's short cyclical segments, however, the enjoyment of rapid repetition, with short melodic phrases and breaks that animate the groove, draws attention away from progress through the ABCD form of the song and from the even larger-scale theme and variation experience of form. This results in a momentary suspension of the arrangement's forward motion through time, where the listener is drawn to participate physically and verbally in the exciting rhythmic and melodic conversation.

The call-and-response jam represents the most obvious connection between Panorama music and the carnival *lavways* that steelbands once accompanied on the road. Many other modern steelband conventions, however—such as the technical demands on the players, the lack of improvisation, and performing on stage instead of on the road—represent important changes that Panorama has brought about in steelband performance and in the role steelbands play in carnival. Above all, Panorama has exalted the role of the steelband arranger, and arrangers have replaced tuners as the stars of the modern steelbands. Many arrangers are associated with particular bands—Jit Samaroo with Renegades, for example, or Boogsie Sharpe with Phase II—but successful arrangers are in high demand, and most have arranged for more than one steelband. In addition to Samaroo and Sharpe, the list of Trinidad's most famous active steelband arrangers would also have to include Ray Holman, Clive Bradley, Ken "Professor" Philmore, Robert Greenidge, and Pelham Goddard.

FRAMING TRADITION

It might seem contradictory that a competition established to promote local tradition has produced such radical changes in the way steelbands make music. Traditions, however, do not stand still. On the contrary, traditions are re-enacted every year at carnival time and are newly conceived in every generation. Like the masquerade competitions sponsored by merchants in the early twentieth century (Chapter 1), Panorama performances can be seen as a process of negotiation between different views and as a discovery of new possibilities.

Through Panorama, government and private businesses have taken an active role in promoting the steelband as a national art form. Trinidad's first prime minister, Eric Williams, was known to pressure large companies into sponsoring steelbands. The Amoco oil company (sponsor of the Renegades), the West Indian Tobacco Company (Desperados), and the Solo beverage company (Harmonites) are a few of the many businesses that have attached their names and logos to steelbands and have provided money for instruments, arrangers' fees, and other expenses. In addition to concerns they may have about cultural identity, politicians and businesspeople recognize that their support for the steelbands will win them votes and clients in the neighborhoods where these bands are located. In this pattern of steelband patronage we can see another example of the intertwining of politics and art that historically characterizes carnival.

In addition to affording steelbands more prestige and exposure, Panorama has also put them under increased pressure to accommodate the musical ideas of other groups. The rules of the Panorama competition, and their enforcement by judges with formal musical training, have set new musical standards for steelbands to meet. The rule that all the steelbands should play a calypso from the current year, for example, was resented by many steelband musicians, particularly when Panorama came to consume more and more of the steelbands' time and energy. A few arrangers tried to circumvent this rule by writing their own compositions. Ray Holman was the first to do this with Starlift steelband in 1972, and Boogsie Sharpe followed suit with his band, Phase II Pan Groove. Even these so-called own tunes, however, have only been successful in Panorama when they were first popularized in a vocal version on records, CDs, and radio before carnival—just like the calypsoes of the calypsonians. The Panorama competition therefore has played a significant role in reinforcing the ideological association between the "national instrument" and the "national music"—an association that was less obvious in the early days of the steelband.

On the other hand, official efforts to influence steelband repertoire have had many unanticipated results because arrangers, players, audiences, and judges all have had their own kind of input into Panorama. When competition organizers required that steelbands limit their Panorama repertoire to calypso, the musicians responded by arranging calypsoes in ever more complicated ways, introducing many musical ideas (about form, texture, harmony, etc.) that they had learned from classical music. The judges, most of whom are not steelband musicians, are often thought to favor this "classical" approach to calypso in Panorama—a somewhat ironic and unforeseen development for a competition that was meant to promote "local" music. The audience, for its part, wants excitement. The faster and louder the bands play, the more the audience seems to like it, and the sweetness of timbre and dynamic contrast that are so prized in some contexts may not survive the hammering of the musicians as they "beat pan" for the frenzied Panorama crowds. Arrangers must also accommodate the expectations of the players, who enjoy dramatic and virtuosic music that allows them to strut and prance in the glory of the bright stage. The impact of a Panorama performance is made both through the sound of the music and through the visual spectacle of the players' movements, their colorful matching outfits, the hundreds of chromed and decorated pans, the dancing flag-wavers, and the excited crowds.

∽

For better or for worse, Panorama has brought about obvious changes in the repertoire and style of Trinidad steelbands, as well as in their financing and organization. At the same time, however, Panorama performances continue to manifest long-standing carnival traditions of rivalry, boasting, masquerade, and festivity that have adapted and persisted in a new context. This relationship between innovation and tradition is an important dynamic in virtually all musical traditions, and in the next chapter I explore it in relation to some modern genres of carnival music.

CHAPTER 6

Bacchanal Time

∾

"Bacchanal" is a word for wild revelry that derives from the name of Bacchus, the Roman god of wine. Trinidadian carnival is a sensual bacchanal—an exuberance of movement, sound, and display for which calypso, steelband, and other kinds of carnival music provide a vital impulse. For example, the song "Bacchanal Time," sung by Super Blue in 1993, exorts masqueraders to "jump up," "start to wave," "express yourself," "wine" (wind your waist), and generally enjoy themselves without restraint (Figure 6.1). Trinidadians also use the word "bacchanal" to refer to mischief and corruption in politics, cheating on a lover, or anything that creates confusion and disorder. These kinds of political and social bacchanals are lampooned in masquerade and calypso every year at carnival. And since the 1980s, the profusion of new carnival music genres has been a kind of bacchanal in itself, giving rise to all kinds of disputes about value and authenticity in music. This chapter gives examples of some of the most significant new genres of music that have grown out of calypso in recent years—soca, rapso, ragga soca, and chutney soca—considering both their musical conventions and the ideas that people associate with them.

SOCA

The term "soca" is commonly said to derive from "soul calypso," suggesting a blend of African American and Trinidadian music. Lord Shorty, who coined the term in the late 1970s, spelled it "sokah" and said it was meant to be a fusion of calypso with East Indian music. There are differing opinions as to how soca should be defined, and some would argue that it is really just another kind of calypso, as calypso has always been sung in different styles. Nonetheless, the majority (though not necessarily all) of the songs that are popular for dancing on the streets during Trinidadian carnival would be described today as soca

FIGURE 6.1 *A couple wining down low together, Port of Spain, 1993.*

rather than calypso. The supremacy of soca on the road was firmly established in the early 1990s by the calypsonian Super Blue (Figure 6.2), who sang the most popular road march three years in a row, establishing a new model for carnival music that featured instructions to the dancers, faster tempos, and energetic rhythmic vocalizations. This is music that is made for dancing and pleasure, complementing and overlapping with the word play and social commentary of calypso in the tent. As these two kinds of music have come to be perceived more differently, the term "calypso" has tended more and more to be reserved for the music that is sung in the calypso tents, while "soca" has been associated with the road and with fetes.

FIGURE 6.2 *Super Blue (Austin Lyons). From the liner notes to* Soca Matrix, *Rituals Music CO7000.*

One of the most obvious differences between calypso and soca is in the nature of each genre's lyrics. Calypso for the tent privileges word play and message over dance and is generally characterized by a narrative text. This means that each phrase in a calypso is packed full of words, and the phrases and strophes build to tell a story. In contrast, soca lyrics are usually built in short phrases that don't always form a coherent narrative and that are as important for their rhythmic drive and excitement as they are for their meanings. Super Blue's "Pump It Up" (CD track 1), the most popular road march of the 2000 carnival, is a good example of the use of lyrics for rhythmic effect. Notice the passages where he simply repeats a word—for example "heat, heat, heat"; "wine, wine, wine"; or "pump, pump, pump." He also sings without words to add energy to the music—for example, the high-pitched "oo's" after the repetitions of "I wish I could wine on you," as well as other rhythmic exclamations.

Soca lyrics also tend to use a call-and-response structure with greater frequency than calypso does, in order to generate crowd participation and rhythmic energy. This can be heard, for example, in the part of "Pump It Up" where Super Blue's short phrases are answered by a repeated chorus of "pump up!" that dancers on the street can sing along with the recorded song:

This is carnival
Pump up!
The original
Pump up!
When you hear the brass,
Pump up!
Let me see your mas'
Pump up!

In addition to lyrics, the techniques of studio production in modern soca may also distinguish it from calypso. The electronic snare and other studio effects (heard especially in the section of "Pump It Up" in which Super Blue repeats the words "soca matrix") are sounds that cannot be reproduced easily in the calypso tent using a house band of live instrumentalists. This reliance on synthesized sound and studio recording means that Super Blue's music tends to sound best when it is played on a CD, rather than in live tent performances. During carnival, recorded music like this is played on sound systems with huge speakers, often mounted on moving flatbeds or DJ trucks (Figure 6.3). The power of the low frequencies these speakers put out is particularly important to the aesthetic of modern soca, which features pounding bass lines that are *felt* as much as they are heard. Also notice that percussion (much of it synthesized) is more foregrounded in "Pump It Up" than in most of the calypso recordings in your Listening Examples.

A few particular rhythms are sometimes regarded as markers of soca style, in contrast to calypso. For example, the bass line in "Pump It Up" does not have the "on-beat" feel that you can hear in an older calypso such as "Jean and Dinah." Instead it plays an off-beat pattern [(1), <u>2-and</u>, (3), <u>4-and</u>, as I described for Phase II's "Back Line" (Activity 4.5)]. This rhythm is reinforced by the kick drum (the deep, thumping drum of the drumset) producing the off-beat bass feel that is commonly associated with soca. However, many calypso songs also use this rhythm (e.g. Singing Sandra's "Caribbean Man Part 2," CD track 10) , which underlines the difficulty of defining soca stylistically.

Indeed, in arguments about the relative value of calypso and soca (which take place on the radio, in newspapers, and in conversations be-

FIGURE 6.3   *A DJ truck surrounded by a dancing crowd moves slowly down a Port of Spain street, 1989.*

tween friends) Trinidadians make a variety of ideological distinctions between these genres that may be at least as important as the sound of the music. Partisans of calypso, for example, argue that calypso is Trinidad's national music and that it is important to preserve musical conventions that have a long history in Trinidad; partisans of soca, on the other hand, argue that tradition has to change to stay alive and that mixing calypso with foreign styles is a legitimate innovation. Calypso partisans argue that the tradition of word play and storytelling give calypso a special status of "oral literature," while soca partisans contend that dance and festivity are as important as literature. Calypso partisans may see money as a corrupting influence, while soca partisans counter that calypsonians need to make a living and that Trinidadians can take pride in seeing some of their musicians enjoying international success. Whether and where people draw boundaries between these genres is therefore influenced not only by musical sound and style, but also by how people conceive of generational differences, national culture, the music industry, and the globalization of culture. Similar issues are at stake in the definition of the more recent popular genres of rapso, ragga soca, and chutney soca.

RAPSO

Like the word "soca," "rapso" is understood to imply the fusion of calypso with another style of music, in this case rap. But rap and calypso also can be regarded as related variants in the Man of Words tradition sharing a common African heritage. Indeed, in the early 1970s, even before rap was recognized as a genre in the United States, the calypsonian Lancelot Lane made recordings in a style of rhythmic speech that some Trinidadians see as an important precedent for rap. Rapso, then, builds on the same tradition of verbal artistry and rhythmic performance that produced the carnival *chantwell* and the calypsonian. It also represents a connection between the music of Trinidadian youth and the contemporary speech-song styles of rap in the United States and dance hall in Jamaica.

Rapso was created in the 1970s by young Trinidadians who were interested in exploring and affirming their African cultural roots. In the late 1960s there was widespread discontent with the failure of Trinidad's newly independent government to deliver on its promises of economic and social change. Many young people, especially students at the University of the West Indies, framed their protests in the racial terms of the Black Power movement that was taking place simultaneously in the United States. In 1970 some of the armed forces even staged a brief revolt in order to demonstrate solidarity with the movement. This was a period of social and political turmoil unprecedented in the modern history of Trinidad.

Although the prime minister of Trinidad and the majority of government officials were black, Black Power advocates complained that the government was perpetuating a colonial economic and social system. One of the goals of the Black Power movement was to promote African and Afro-Trinidadian cultural forms. In particular, many young people participated in drumming ensembles in which they learned

Afro-Trinidadian folk forms such as the *bongo* and the *bele*, ritual drumming of the Orisha religion, and various other styles from Africa. Early rapso performances of Lancelot Lane and other innovators were often characterized by this kind of drumming and by a strong social and political consciousness.

Since the 1980s, the leading figure in the rapso movement has been "Brother Resistance" (a.k.a. Lutalo Masimba—Figure 6.4). Brother Resistance brought rapso into the calypso tents in the 1980s, made recordings, and organized rapso concerts in conjunction with carnival to pop-

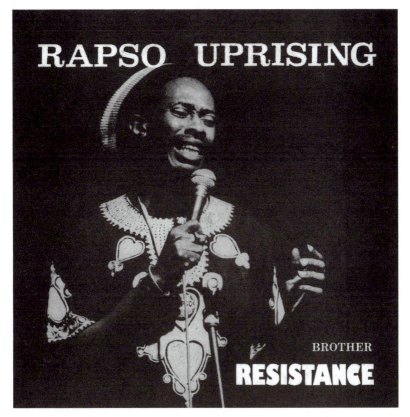

FIGURE 6.4   *Brother Resistance (Lutalo Masimba). Album cover from* Rapso Uprising *Rhythm Distribution Network RDN 021.*

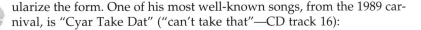

ularize the form. One of his most well-known songs, from the 1989 carnival, is "Cyar Take Dat" ("can't take that"—CD track 16):

I work my finger to the bone for me country
I squeeze blood out of stone for me country
The people in authority
mashing up me family
So much a years that we sweat and toil
Is we blood and tears what till the soil
But we still suffering today
And we children can't see the way, hey
I wake up in the morning and is unemployment
I cyar take dat
I wake up in the morning and it's more retrenchment
I cyar take dat
When they going to stop all this humiliation
I cyar take dat
Wake up in the morning more frustration
I cyar take dat...No!
Ain't taking that, so
People ain't taking that . . .

While the message of this song has precedent in the calypso tradition of social and political commentary, it is different from a calypso like Chalkdust's "Chauffeur Wanted" in at least two ways. First of all, it is extremely serious in its tone, having none of the humor that calypsonians usually use to couch their political messages. Second, its message is phrased in universal terms, rather than in terms of specific people, places, and events in Trinidad. This reflects the song's connection to an international consciousness of Black Power and social progress. Like the reggae songs of Jamaica's Bob Marley, rapso lyrics often speak an international language of social protest and consciousness-raising; in contrast, the power of the calypsonian lies in exposing and embarassing specific individuals and institutions in his own society. The instrumental accompaniment of "Cyar Take Dat" also connects to an international black music aesthetic. The "heavy" feel of the bass and percussion and the horn arranging are more akin to the Afro-Beat of Nigerian singer Fela Anikulapo Kuti (also known internationally for his songs of African pride and strident social/political criticism) than they are to calypso or soca.

While rapso songs such as "Cyar Take Dat" might seem out of step with the prevailing aesthetics of carnival song and festivity, Brother Resistance and others nonetheless have worked hard to popularize rapso in conjunction with carnival. Their effort reflects the importance of carnival as a showcase for local culture. Rapso's inclusion in carnival gives it the status of a "national" art form, akin to calypso, steelband, or masquerade. The performance and recording of rapso at carnival time also reflect the seasonal nature of Trinidadian popular music. It is difficult to market recordings and performances of local music outside of the carnival season because many Trinidadians listen more to U.S. and other international popular music during the rest of the year. Rapso today is stylistically diverse, and younger rapso artists such as Kindred and 3 Canal (as well as Brother Resistance himself in recent years) tend to use instrumental arrangements that are suited to carnival dancing even as they push serious social and political messages.

RAGGA SOCA

The term "ragga soca" references yet another fusion of musical styles, this time between soca and Jamaican music. Ragga is a term used in the United Kingdom for what is called dance hall music in Jamaica (ragga comes from "raggamuffin," a name that ghetto youth have given themselves). Dance hall music developed at dances where DJs played records on sound systems and improvised over them in a speech-song style. It is a close cousin to hip-hop music (rap) in the Unite States, and indeed many of the innovators of hip-hop have Jamaican roots and were influenced by the Jamaican sound systems.

The appeal of dance hall music has been especially strong for Trinidadian youth since the 1980s, but the popularity of Jamaican music generally, and Jamaican style, dates to the international success of Bob Marley and other reggae musicians in the 1970s. Their social criticism and Rastafarian spirituality (symbolized most vividly by the long dreadlock hairstyle) had a strong appeal in other islands of the English-speaking Caribbean. In the 1980s, however, the Jamaican dance hall style—a party music whose themes of sex and gangsterism contrasted with the social or spiritual messages of many reggae songs—became extremely popular with Trinidadian youth. Trinidadians refer to this style of music as "dub" (an erroneous reference, from the Jamaican point of view, since dub music and dub poetry in Jamaica are different from dance hall music), and its pounding, repetitive bass lines have an inescapable presence on the airwaves, on the streets where vendors hawk tapes and

CDs, at neighborhood "blocos" and other dances, and (until police began to crack down on it as a nuisance) in the mini-van "maxi-taxis" that ply the roads all over Trinidad.

Many older Trinidadians regard dub as a form of noise pollution, as a foreign import that threatens local calypso, and as music that is melodically and lyrically impoverished, or even degenerate. Dub, or dance hall, and its Trinidadian cousin ragga soca, are therefore very much a youth music in Trinidad. Although much of the dub that first became

FIGURE 6.5 *School girls delight to Denise Belfon's performance at a free concert in Port of Spain (Nicole Drayton).*

popular in Trinidad was recorded by Jamaican dance hall stars such as Shabba Ranks and Buju Banton, some young Trinidadian artists, such as General Grant, also have made successful recordings in this style and have begun to move from imitation of Jamaican music toward a style that is distinctively Trinidadian. In the 1990s some Trinidadian artists began to refer to their music as "ragga soca," drawing attention to their interest in a fusion of Jamaican and Trinidadian style and challenging the notion that dance hall music is a threat to local culture.

Denise Belfon's recording of "Burnin'" (CD track 17) is a good example of this fusion. The singer who interjects responses to Belfon's lyrics and who is heard by himself at the end of this excerpt speaks with a Jamaican accent, in the speech-song style called "toasting" that Jamaican DJs use (Figure 6.5). Some of Belfon's own lyrics are delivered without any attempt at imitating Jamaican speech, but when she sings the passage beginning with "Spin the dub," she falls into a kind rhythmic/melodic pattern (using just two or three distinct pitches) that is borrowed from dance hall speech-song:

> *Spin the dub-a cause I know it ignite-a*
> *Feel the heat cause I know that it rise-a*
> *Work me body and I know that it burnin'*
> *Burnin, burnin, burnin*

The bass and percussion accompaniment in this recording reflects the repetitive and bass-heavy sound of dance hall instrumental tracks, but the rhythms give it a touch of Trinidadian feel. For example, "Burnin'" features an off-beat soca rhythm of the bass (as described in Activity 4.5), and the accents of the snare drums match the calypso strum rhythm in Figure A of Activity 3.6.

In addition to the dance hall–soca fusion, another trend that "Burnin'" exemplifies is the changing role of women in Trinidadian music. In Chapter 2 I discussed how Singing Sandra challenged the male calypsonian's perspective on society by calling attention to the "Caribbean Man's" sexism and domestic irresponsibility. Sandra speaks in the moral tones of a church elder, of a mother and wife. Denise Belfon, by contrast, takes no such moral stance, instead celebrating her sex appeal both in her lyrics and in her dancing on stage. Some might argue that she is pandering to the sexual objectification of women that is such a dominant theme in calypso and soca, but the important difference in "Burnin'" is that the woman is not an object of man's desire but instead is expressing her own sexual desire and her own power to judge men sexually:

When he's hot he's hot
Oh yeah!
And if he's not you know it
If he's not you know,
Cause I like men when they steamin' hot,
Cause I like men when they steamin' hot

Considered in the context of Trinidadian popular culture (think, for example, of the Mighty Sparrow's warning to "the girls in town" that "the Yankees gone and Sparrow take over now!"), Belfon's challenge to male sexual power and control is at least as threatening and revolutionary as Sandra's moral criticism is. This explains why Denise Belfon is so popular among young Trinidadian women, and it shows how serious ideas and values can be at stake in songs that deal with sex and pleasure.

CHUTNEY SOCA

While the musical fusions in rapso and ragga soca tend to draw attention to the relationship between Trinidadian and foreign musical styles, chutney soca brings together two Trinidadian cultures that are often perceived as distinct or even antagonistic—Indian and Afro-Trinidadian (also referred to as "creole"). The word "chutney" refers to the sweet and spicy pickles used as condiments in Indian cuisine. Chutney music is said to derive from a genre of songs, characterized by ribald humor, that are sung by Indian women for a bride-to-be the night before her wedding. Chutney music today, however, is not particularly associated with this context. Instead it is a music for social dancing whose popularity has spread from Trinidad to other Caribbean countries and to Indian diaspora communities as far away as South Africa.

The term "traditional" chutney today refers to the instrumentation of harmonium, *dholak*, and *dhantal* (Figure 1.7). For dancing, however, people generally prefer modern chutney. Modern chutney ensembles often retain the *dholak*, if only for symbolism, but they also feature electric bass and guitar, drumset, and keyboard. Their musical style is characterized by a blend of Indian folk melodies with Indian film music style and Trinidadian soca and calypso rhythms. Chutney music, both traditional and modern, is commonly performed at dances where working-class people pay to enjoy themselves on a weekend evening. Dancers at chutney concerts enjoy wining their waists in the sexually suggestive fashion of Afro-Trinidadian carnival dancing, but they also use many gestures, especially with the hands, that are patterned on Indian film dancing and other Indian styles of dance (Figure 6.6).

FIGURE 6.6   *Dancing to chutney music at the Sugar Cane Workers Union Building in Couva, 1993.*

The use of "chutney soca" as a genre name is not much older than the Chutney Soca Monarch competition itself, which began in 1996. Since modern chutney (as opposed to "traditional" chutney accompanied by harmonium, *dholak*, and *dhantal*) already fuses soca with Indian music, the distinction between chutney and chutney soca is difficult to define. Both use the same instrumentation, both fuse Indian and Caribbean musical elements, both may be sung in Hindi or in English, and both are danced to in the same way. The new name has as much to do with efforts to bring chutney into carnival as it has to do with distinctions of musical style. The need for a separate Chutney Soca competition was underscored, for example, by an incident at the 1996 Soca

Monarch competition in which Indo-Trinidadian singer Sonny Mann was booed off the stage by audience members who felt that his song, "Lotay La," did not belong in a soca show.

Chutney music, like rapso, has its origins outside of carnival, and efforts to integrate it into carnival reflect a desire on the part of Indo-Trinidadians to be included in the annual showcase of Trinidad's "national" culture. This more inclusive vision of the national culture has received increased government support since 1995, when the UNC won the parliamentary elections for the first time and Basdeo Panday became Trinidad's first prime minister of Indian descent. Indo-Trinidadian interest in cultural representation was reflected at the Chutney Soca Monarch competition I attended in 2000, where the singers were accompanied by elaborate dances and dramatic representations, many of which had patriotic themes and included images of reconciliation between Afro-Trinidadians and Indo-Trinidadians (e.g., showing one another how to dance in new ways).

The most successful chutney soca singer in Trinidad is Rikki Jai (Figure 6.7). Jai began his career as a calypsonian, bursting onto the carnival scene in 1989 with a hit song called "Sumintra" about an Indian girl who prefers soca over Indian film music. In the song, Sumintra refuses to be defined in

FIGURE 6.7   *Rikki Jai. CD cover from* Chutney Soca Monarch.

stereotypical ethnic terms and proclaims her "Trinbagonian" identity (a citizen of Trinidad and Tobago is called a "Trinbagonian"). The instrumentation and musical style lend a mild Indian flavor to the soca. The success of "Sumintra" coincided with the rising popularity of the female Indian calypsonian Drupatee and seemed to promise new opportunities for Indian singers and Indian music in carnival. It proved difficult, however, for Jai to gain acceptance as a calypsonian, and in recent years he has mainly performed chutney soca for Indian audiences, winning the Chutney Soca Monarch competition in 1998, 1999, 2001, and 2002. Drupatee has remained more prominent on the calypso scene, but as an Indian singer in a genre that is strongly associated with Afro-Trinidadian performers and audiences, she fights an uphill battle to get work and recognition.

In 1998 Rikki Jai had some crossover success again with the song "Dulahin," which was played on the radio and on the road at carnival (CD track 18). One aspect of this song that appealed to carnival dancers was the series of rhythmic breaks, a device commonly used in soca to create excitement and dance energy. Compare the effect of Rikki Jai's break in "Dulahin" at the words "Bélé she flat, bélé she flat, bélé she flat, flat, flat, flat, flat" with Super Blue's break in "Pump It Up" (CD track 1) at the words "I wish I could, I wish I could, I wish I could, I wish I could wine on you!" (an interruption and then an exciting return of the rhythmic feel, as discussed in Chapter 3).

In general, however, and certainly in comparison to Jai's 1989 hit "Sumintra," "Dulahin" sounds more chutney than soca. The instrumentation is dominated by the harmonium and the *dholak*, while the kick drum, snare, and high hat provide a soca beat in the background. The melody and ornamentation of the harmonium are clearly Indian, and Jai's vocal phrasing (a subtle matter for outsiders but a crucial marker of style for Trinidadians) is not in typical calypso or soca style. Hints of Indian vocal ornament also distinguish his singing style here from calypso singing style (Activity 6.1).

ACTIVITY 6.1: VOCAL ORNAMENT (CD TRACK 18) *Indian music is characterized by sophisticated and extensive use of melodic ornament. In "Dulahin," Rikki Jai makes subtle turns in pitch at the end of certain phrases that are markers of Indian singing style, particularly as heard in Indian films. Listen, for example, to the word "Dulahin" in the chorus, which is ornamented to different degrees each time it is sung, with a*

slight quaver or bend in pitch on the last one or two syllables. Another clear example of this melodic ornament occurs in the phrase "washin' and cookin'" on the "-shin'" syllable.

The lyrics of "Dulahin" also speak of a characteristically Indian predicament, the pressure from parents who want to arrange their childrens' marriages:

> *Me mother only quarrelin' she want me find a dulahin*
> *Me mother only quarrelin' she want me find a dulahin*
> *She want me find a dulahin, she want me find a dulahin,*
> > *She want me find a dulahin*
> *Me mother only quarrelin' she want me find a dulahin*
> *Whole day I limin', whole night I fetin'*
> *Me mother dey home only washin' and cookin'*
> *Me mother only quarrelin' she want me find a dulahin*

"Dulahin" is a Hindi word for bride. Many older Indian Trinidadians grew up hearing Hindi (or the more regionally specific dialect called Bhojpuri) in their homes, and even younger ones who don't really understand Hindi learn to sing along with the lyrics of Hindi film songs. Rikki Jai's mother writes the lyrics for the Hindi songs he sings, and Jai prides himself on his pronunciation, even though he doesn't speak or understand much Hindi himself. Chutney songs also include Trinidadian idioms that Indians use as freely as creoles (examples in this song include "bélé," meaning to beat; or "liming," meaning hanging out and socializing).

The song "Dulahin," like the genre of chutney soca in general, is a fascinating hybrid of languages and musical styles. While some creoles would still dismiss it as something "Indian" that does not belong in carnival, others have responded with interest and enjoyment to Indian influences in carnival music. The barrier between these musical aesthetics is therefore under continuous assault from both sides of the Indian-African cultural divide.

DEFINING MUSICAL GENRES

One issue that arises in relation to all of these new types of carnival music is the problem of defining boundaries between genres. It is not always easy to draw a distinction between calypso and soca, or between rapso and ragga soca, or between chutney and chutney soca solely on the basis of a particular musical trait such as a rhythm or an instrumentation. Sometimes social styles and identities, or the political agendas associated with certain genres, are as important to people as musical sound. To take an example from U.S. pop music, a "new country" song might *sound* a lot like rock and roll, but the hats and boots and line dancing at a nightclub are clues that help us identify it as country. Some "disco" songs might have been called rhythm and blues if they hadn't become associated with discotheques, polyester pants, and mirror balls in the 1970s. And some of the "alternative" music of the 1990s sounded a lot like the Beatles, or other music of the 1960s and 1970s, so what made people think of it as something new and different? Musicians and listeners attach importance to genre boundaries, but these boundaries are difficult to determine for someone who is not familiar with the way people talk about and participate in music and with the opinions, values, and identities—what we could refer to broadly as "ideologies"—people attach to certain songs and styles.

Many such ideologies are important to the distinctions Trinidadians make between genres of carnival music. Traditionalists complain, for example, that the true calypso is dying, that young people are losing appreciation for their own culture as they imitate the fashions and music of the United States and Jamaica. Progressives counter that calypso must change and grow so that it will be relevant to new generations that are increasingly connected to international popular culture. Women challenge the male-dominated music establishment and assert their own voices and sexuality. East Indians claim their place in carnival through the promotion of chutney soca. Some people conceive of calypso broadly and argue that soca, rapso, ragga soca (though perhaps not chutney soca) should be considered variants of calypso. Others insist on genre distinctions as a way of promoting a certain concept of tradition or a particular type of innovation. Musicians seeking to innovate and make a name for themselves sometimes give new genre names to the style of music they play. These are examples of the social concerns that drive musical innovation and influence the ways that people talk about and relate to different genres of carnival music.

CONCLUSION

Trinidadians argue passionately about whether modern changes in carnival are good or bad. Concepts of tradition and social identify figure prominently in these arguments and are also expressed in carnival per-

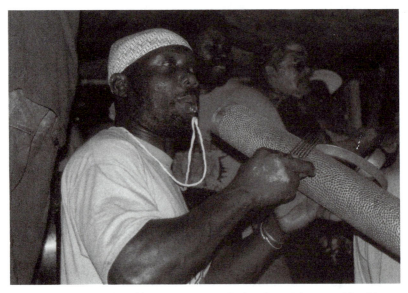

FIGURE 6.8   *Scratcher player in San Juan Rhythm Section (an ensemble of drums, irons, and other nonmelodic percussion instruments) laying down the beat for Jouvert morning mud mas'.*

formances. For example, the *j'ouvert* morning celebration (Chapter 1), in which people play "dirty mas'" (covering themselves in mud or oil) and jump up to the music of a "riddim section" (Figure 6.8) has become increasingly popular in recent years. In addition to being inexpensive fun, many people also celebrate *j'ouvert*'s anti-establishment rebelliousness and grassroots organization as the traditional essence of carnival. On the other hand, thousands of Trinidadians pay expensive costume prices to be seen in one of the big "pretty mas'" bands, and a large majority of these celebrants are women. These women's enthusiasm for commercial costumes and "freeing up" in public is seen by some Trinidadians as a sign of cultural or moral decline, but it also corresponds to their increasing social and economic power in modern Trinidad. Change and controversy, as much as continuity and tradition, have always been and always will be part of the bacchanal of Trinidadian carnival, reflecting the dynamism of a diverse and evolving society. Musicians who respond to carnival's shifting and competing performance contexts make creative innovations and also draw on time-tested techniques to satisfy—and provoke—their listeners.

Glossary

∞

bamboo tamboo: an ensemble of bamboo stamping tubes

bass pan: the steel pan with the lowest register, tuned today in a set of between six and twelve full-sized oil barrels

belaire: a drum dance featuring intricate coordination between dancer and drummer

Bomb competition: a practice especially popular in the 1950s and 1960s in which steelbands played classical music and other foreign compositions in calypso style

bongo: a drum dance often performed at wakes

braid: to weave together different parts in a polyrhythmic texture, as in "braiding the irons"

break: a sudden unison or silence that interrupts a polyrhythmic texture, used to generate excitement

call and response: song form in which the improvisations of a soloist alternate with a repeated refrain sung by a chorus; often used to describe similar relationships in instrumental music

calypso: topical song sung at carnival and other festivals in the English Caribbean

Calypso Monarch competition: annual event associated with Trinidad carnival, dating to the 1950s

calypso tent: a theater, auditorium, or other indoor venue where calypsonians take turns performing for a paying audience

calypsonian: a professional singer of calypso

cellos: a set of three steel pans that plays in a low register, between the bass and the double seconds

chip: to dance down the road with a simple alternating step (from the sound of leather soles scraping on pavement)

chord: a combination of three or more notes that sound together in a particular way, used as harmonic support for a melody

chord progression: a sequence of chords

chromatic: melodic movement by half steps, the smallest interval in the Western diatonic scale

chutney: a Caribbean song genre that mixes East Indian film songs and folk melodies with calypso and soca

circle of fifths: a series of notes (or chords) that are a fifth apart, ending up with the starting note: for example, C-G-D-A-E-B-F#-C#-G#-Eb-Bb-F-C; in Trinidad, the term also refers to a tenor pan in which the notes are organized in this sequence

creole: a person of European descent born in the New World; also used in Trinidad to refer to people of African descent, in distinction to people of East Indian descent

cuatro: a small guitar-type instrument with four strings used to strum chords, from Venezuela

cutter: the improvising part in a polyrhythmic ensemble of drums, bamboo, or irons

cyclical form: a form characterized by fairly rapid repetition of a melody or rhythm, usually with improvised variations

dance hall: a Jamaican style of music in which DJs recite lyrics in a speech-song style over a recorded background track

dhol: a large double ended barrel drum that plays a fixed rhythmic figure to accompany the tassa drum

dholak: a double-ended Indian folk drum held in the lap of a sitting musician; used in Trinidad to accompany chutney singing, as well as other Indian genres

dhantal: a straight metal rod played with a metal beater to give percussive accompaniment to chutney music

DJ truck: a flatbed truck carrying large speakers to broadcast recorded music on the streets during carnival

double seconds: steel pans consisting of two drums, each tuned in a whole tone scale

Festival: see Music Festival

form: the shape of a musical selection; structure

half step: the smallest interval in the Western diatonic scale; for example, on a piano, the distance in pitch between a white key and the adjacent black key

harmonics: high-frequency pitches that are generated above the note played on any musical instrument

harmonium: a portable bellow driven keyboard used in many genres of Indian music

harmony: pitches that sound together; in tonal music, system of functional chords, or chord progressions

Hosay: name used in Trinidad for the Muslim festival of Moharram

instrumentation: instruments used in a musical selection

interval: distance spanned between two pitches

iron: a metal idiophone, typically a brake drum from a car or truck, used as a percussion instrument in Trinidad steelbands

janjh: a pair of hand-held cymbals that are played to accompany tassa drumming

j'ouvert: the pre-dawn festivities on the opening Monday of Trinidad carnival (from the French *jour ouvert*)

kaiso: see calypso

kalenda: a kind of stick-fighting performed in Trinidad, with the accompaniment of singing and drumming; the term is also used elsewhere in the Caribbean (especially in historical references) to refer to neo-African dance music

lavway: a short refrain sung in call-and-response style during carnival

mas': masquerade, costume

meter: regular grouping of beats

Music Festival: a biennial competition in Trinidad dedicated mainly to classical music

octave: an interval in which the frequency of the second note is twice that of the first; musically we hear notes that are one or more octaves apart as the "same note" (e.g., when men and women sing together in unison)

Orisha: a generic term for the gods in the Yoruban culture of West Africa; in Trinidad the term also refers to a neo-African religion, as in "Orisha worship"

pan: a musical instrument made from beating the bottom of an oil drum into a concave bowl and tuning different areas of the surface to different pitches, sounded by striking them with rubber-tipped mallets

Panorama: an annual carnival competition in Trinidad, in which steelbands perform complex arrangements of current calypsoes

panman: a person who plays pan

parang: a genre of Christmas songs sung in Spanish (from the Spanish *parranda*)

phrase: a melodic unit; musical thought

phrasing: in Western music, the way a performer articulates melodic phrases; in Trinidad, the way a performer renders a melody rhythmically

picong: a competitive verbal exchange, usually including insults; in reference to calypsonians, picong refers to such verbal exchanges performed in song

ping pong: onomatopoetic name for an early steel pan

polyrhythm: a musical texture created by performing repeated and contrasting rhythms in an interlocking fashion

rapso: a Trinidadian speech-song genre that draws on both rap and calypso

road march: song for dancing on the road at carnival time

rhythmic feel: the rhythmic character of a song or genre, as created by polyrhythmic interaction between different parts

scale: a set of pitches presented in straight ascending or descending order

soca: a genre of carnival dance music in Trinidad, generally considered a modern derivative of calypso

soca chutney: chutney music with soca influences

steel pan: see pan

steel drum: see pan

strophic form: structure consisting of an entire melody repeated; usually associated with songs in which each new verse of lyrics is set to the same melody

tassa: a small kettle-shaped drum from India with a clay body covered with a tight skin and struck by fine-tipped mallets; accompanied by a large double-ended bass drum

tenor pan: the steel pan with the highest range, made from a single oil barrel

texture: musical relationships among ensemble parts

theme and variation: a musical form in which several melodies are composed over a repeated chord progression

timbre: particular quality of sound; tone color

whole step: a pitch interval equivalent to two half steps

whole tone scale: a scale in which each note is a whole step interval from the last

wine: to dance with a particular style of rotating the waist and pelvis

Resources

∞

Resources provided here include a bibliography, discography, and videography, as well as contact information for the record producers and distributors who generously granted permission for the Listening Examples.

Reading

Abrahams, Roger. 1983. *The Man-of-Words in the West Indies.* Baltimore: Johns Hopkins University Press. A collection of essays describing Afro-Caribbean folk performance in several of the smaller English-speaking islands.

Cowley, John. 1996. *Carnival, Canboulay, and Calypso: Traditions in the Making.* New York: Cambridge University Press. A detailed chronological account of Trinidad carnival in the nineteenth and early twentieth centuries.

Dudley, Shannon. 1996. "Judging by the Beat: Calypso vs. Soca." *Ethnomusicology* 40(2):269–298. Explores the musical differences and similarities between soca and calypso, as suggested by an analysis of "rhythmic feel" and also as perceived by Trinidadians.

———. 2002. "Dropping the Bomb: Steelband Music and Meaning in 1960s Trinidad." *Ethnomusicology* 46(1):135–164. Analyzes various political and aesthetic meanings that people attached to a performance tradition in which foreign music, especially European classical music, was played for carnival dancing.

Goddard, George. 1991. *Forty Years in the Steelbands: 1939–1979.* Edited by Roy D. Thomas. London: Karia Press. Memoirs of one of the steelband movement's most influential leaders.

Hill, Donald. 1993. *Calypso Calaloo: Early Carnival Music in Trinidad.* Gainesville: University Press of Florida. Spans the late nineteenth-century jamette carnival to the emergence of calypso as commercial music, both in Trinidad and abroad, in the first half of the twentieth century; rich in biographical detail. Includes CD.

Hill, Errol. 1972. *The Trinidad Carnival: Mandate for a National Theater.* Austin: University of Texas Press. A useful overview of the history and different performance genres of Trinidad carnival.

Liverpool, Hollis. 2001. *Rituals of Power and Rebellion: The Carnival Tradition in Trinidad and Tobago, 1763–1962.* Chicago, Jamaica, and London: Research Associates School Times Publications/Frontline Distribution International Inc. A history of carnival through the eyes of someone who is both scholar and performer (the author is calypsonian Mighty Chalkdust), analyzing the political meaning and impact of carnival performances.

Manuel, Peter. 2000. *East Indian Music in the West Indies: Tan-Singing, Chutney, and the Making of Indo-Caribbean Culture.* Philadelphia: Temple University Press. Focuses mainly on a classical style of Indian singing in Trinidad and Guyana; one chapter covers chutney music, including its relationship to Trinidad carnival. Includes CD.

Ottley, Rudolph. 1995. *Calypsonians from Then to Now, Parts 1 & 2.* Trinidad: Author. A collection of interviews with prominent calypsonians.

Rohlehr, Gordon. 1990. *Calypso and Society in Pre-Independence Trinidad.* St. Augustine, Trinidad: Author. A detailed chronological analysis of early calypso, relating song tests to contemporary events.

Stuempfle, Stephen. 1995. *The Steelband Movement: The Forging of a National Art in Trinidad and Tobago.* Philadelphia: University of Pennsylvania Press. A comprehensive history of the steelband movement.

Viewing

"Steelbands of Trinidad." Distributed by Villon Films, 77 West 28 Avenue, Vancouver, V5Y 2K7, Canada. 604-879-6042. Includes interviews with several Trinidad steelband musicians and footage of Panorama performances and rehearsals.

"Mas fever," Distributed by University of California Extension Center for Media and Independent Learning, 2000 Center St., Fourth Floor, Berkeley, CA 94704. A general overview of Trinidad carnival, produced in conjunction with the Smithsonian Institution's Caribbean Festival Arts program.

"One Hand Don't Clap," Distributed by Rhapsody Films http://www.cinemaweb.com/rhapsody/. A documentary on calypso which includes Kitchener performing "Pan in A Minor," and performances by other calypsonians.

Listening

Only a few CDs are cited here for their broad representation of Trinidad carnival music. For further references, see the recording citations in the Listening Examples and visit the Web sites of artists and distributors who contributed to this volume, listed at the end of this chapter.

Mighty Sparrow and Lord Kitchener: 16 Carnival Hits. Ice Records. This is a good beginning collection of two of Trinidad's most important calypsonians. Ice Records also has other compilations of Kitchener and Sparrow, as well as other historical and contemporary recordings (see contact information at the end of this chapter).

Calypso Awakening. Smithsonian Folkways Recordings SFW CD 40453, 2000. A selection of recordings made both live in the tent and in the studio by Emory Cook in Trinidad in the late 1950s; especially good for the calypsoes of Lord Melody and Might Sparrow, several of which respond to each other. Also includes other calypsonians as well as a steelband and brassband. Many other Trinidad recordings from the Cook collection (e.g., old steelbands) can also be purchased from Smithsonian Folkways (see contact information at the end of this chapter).

Enhanced CD. Rituals Music CO5698, 1998. Includes modern performers in a variety of styles, from soca to rapso to Indian-African fusion. Rituals Music is a good source generally for modern Trinidadian artists and styles; each year they put out CD of carnival hits titled *Caribbean Party Rhythms.*

Calypso Pioneers. Rounder Records ROUN1039, 1989. An interesting collection of early twentieth-century Trinidad carnival music recordings, including both vocal and instrumental tracks. Rounder also has some other calypso collections.

Caribbean Voyage. Rounder Records, 1999. A series comprised of recordings made by Alan Lomax in 1962, including some in Trinidad. These include some recordings of East Indian music.

Caribbean Carnival Series. Delos. A collection of Panorama steelband performances grouped by year, recorded by Simeon Sandiford. Sandiford has also produced several of his own collections (see contact information at the end of this chapter).

Artist and Distributor Contact Information

Ice Records, Bayleys Plantation,
St. Philip, Barbados,
www.icerecords.com

Rikki Jai, rikkijai@yahoo.com

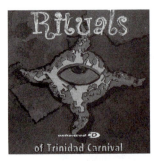

Rituals Music, 5 Longden
Street, Port of Spain, Trinidad
W.I., www.ritualsmusic.com,
868-625-3262

SANCH, 16 Riverside Road,
Curepe, Trinidad W.I.,
868-663-1384,
sanch@carib-link.com

Rounder Records, One Camp
Street, Cambridge, MA 02140,
www.rounder.com,
800-443-4727

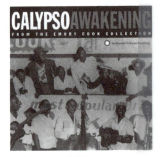

Smithsonian Folkways
Recordings, Department 0607,
Washington, DC 20073-0607,
www.folkways.si.edu,
800-410-9815

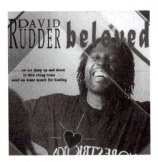

David Rudder,
www.davidrudder.co.tt

Straker's Record World,
242 Utica Avenue, Brooklyn,
NY 11213, 718-756-0040

Index

∞